WINNING IN TRAFFIC COURT MADE E-Z

MADE E-Z PRODUCTS, Inc.
Deerfield Beach, Florida / www.MadeE-Z.com

Winning in Traffic Court Made E-Z™
Copyright 2000 Made E-Z Products, Inc.
Printed in the United States of America

MADE E-Z
PRODUCTS

384 South Military Trail
Deerfield Beach, FL 33442
Tel. 954-480-8933
Fax 954-480-8906
http://www.MadeE-Z.com

1 2 3 4 5 6 7 8 9 10   CPC   R   10 9 8 7 6 5 4 3 2

Winning in Traffic Court Made E-Z™

Important Notice

Limited warranty and disclaimer

This self-help product is intended to be used by the consumer for his/her own benefit. It may not be reproduced in whole or in part, resold or used for commercial purposes without written permission from the publisher. In addition to copyright violations, the unauthorized reproduction and use of this product to benefit a second party may be considered the unauthorized practice of law.

This product is designed to provide authoritative and accurate information in regard to the subject matter covered. However, the accuracy of the information is not guaranteed, as laws and regulations may change or be subject to differing interpretations. Consequently, you may be responsible for following alternative procedures, or using material or forms different from those supplied with this product. It is strongly advised that you examine the laws of your state before acting upon any of the material contained in this product.

As with any matter, common sense should determine whether you need the assistance of an attorney. We urge you to consult with an attorney, qualified estate planner, or tax professional, or to seek any other relevant expert advice whenever substantial sums of money are involved, you doubt the suitability of the product you have purchased, or if there is anything about the product that you do not understand including its adequacy to protect you. Even if you are completely satisfied with this product, we encourage you to have your attorney review it.

Neither the author, publisher, distributor nor retailer are engaged in rendering legal, accounting or other professional services. Accordingly, the publisher, author, distributor and retailer shall have neither liability nor responsibility to any party for any loss or damage caused or alleged to be caused by the use of this product.

Copyright Notice

The purchaser of this guide is hereby authorized to reproduce in any form or by any means, electronic or mechanical, including photocopying, all forms and documents contained in this guide, provided it is for non-profit, educational or private use. Such reproduction requires no further permission from the publisher and/or payment of any permission fee.

The reproduction of any form or document in any other publication intended for sale is prohibited without the written permission of the publisher. Publication for nonprofit use should provide proper attribution to Made E-Z Products.

Table of contents

How to use this guide

The Made E-Z™ guides can help you achieve an important legal objective conveniently, efficiently and economically. But it is important to properly use this guide if you are to avoid later difficulties.

◆ Carefully read all information, warnings and disclaimers concerning the legal forms in this guide. If after thorough examination you decide that you have circumstances that are not covered by the forms in this guide, or you do not feel confident about preparing your own documents, consult an attorney.

◆ Complete each blank on each legal form. Do not skip over inapplicable blanks or lines intended to be completed. If the blank is inapplicable, mark "N/A" or "None" or use a dash. This shows you have not overlooked the item.

◆ Always use pen or type on legal documents—never use pencil.

◆ Avoid erasures and "cross-outs" on final documents. Use photocopies of each document as worksheets, or as final copies. All documents submitted to the court must be printed on one side only.

◆ Correspondence forms may be reproduced on your own letterhead if you prefer.

◆ Whenever legal documents are to be executed by a partnership or corporation, the signatory should designate his or her title.

◆ It is important to remember that on legal contracts or agreements between parties all terms and conditions must be clearly stated. Provisions may not be enforceable unless in writing. All parties to the agreement should receive a copy.

◆ Instructions contained in this guide are for your benefit and protection, so follow them closely.

◆ You will find a glossary of useful terms at the end of this guide. Refer to this glossary if you encounter unfamiliar terms.

◆ Always keep legal documents in a safe place and in a location known to your spouse, family, personal representative or attorney.

Introduction to Winning in Traffic Court Made E-Z™

Congratulations! Simply by picking up this book, you have changed your luck and improved the odds that you can and will win in traffic court.

Millions of traffic citations will be issued this year. The resulting revenue alone is a strong incentive for continued strict enforcement of traffic laws by cities and states. Some traffic officers are evaluated in part by the tickets they write. This adds up to trouble for you if you are on the receiving end of a traffic citation.

There are often good reasons to fight your ticket in court. Challenging your ticket offers the best way to minimize your point count. Most states keep and share records of a driver's points, which reflect the number and severity of his or her violations. The accumulation of points—often a matter of public record—can lead to a suspended license. It is also used by insurance companies to raise rates, and by potential employers concerned about liability for their employees' negligent driving. By minimizing the points you accumulate, a successful defense in traffic court can greatly simplify your life.

Those involved in traffic law enforcement, from meter maids to judges, expect you to plead guilty, pay your ticket, accept your penalty, and maintain the status quo. But by reading this guide you are saying that you won't be victimized by the system, and you increase the likelihood that you will be *Winning in Traffic Court*.

If you handle yourself better the next time the police pull you over in traffic, this guide has succeeded. If you get a warning that could have been a ticket, or a ticket that could have been an arrest, this guide has succeeded. If you decide to fight a ticket because you are innocent, or you want to lower the number of points of your penalty, or you simply want to see the system work, this guide has succeeded. If, after reading this book, you decide to plead guilty and pay the price, your decision is an informed one, and this guide has succeeded.

Only you can define success when it comes to fighting in traffic court. This guide can help you achieve it.

Avoiding a traffic ticket

1

Chapter 1

Avoiding a traffic ticket

D1435751

What you'll find in this chapter:

⟾ Avoid getting stopped four ways

⟾ What to do at an accident scene

⟾ Avoid a ticket even if stopped

⟾ Always carry proper papers

⟾ Be polite and in control

What's the best way to beat a ticket? Avoid getting one!

> ⚠ **CAUTION** Most drivers who are stopped invite police scrutiny because of the vehicle they drive or the way they drive.

Your chances of being stopped by a police officer are greatly reduced when you avoid attention. You can reduce your chances of being stopped with these four simple steps:

1) Inspect your vehicle

Periodically check your vehicle to make sure it is in good repair. Turn on your lights to see that they all work, particularly your brake lights and turn signals. Replace bald tires and cracked windows that draw attention to your vehicle. Watch for outdated or improperly displayed license plates or stickers. Police officers are trained to spot improper equipment, so keep your vehicle in good repair and you'll avoid drawing unwelcome attention.

---

2) Drive defensively

Be aware of your surroundings. Most traffic citations are received within 20 miles of the driver's home or work. Police position themselves in areas of "selected enforcement," or where frequent infractions occur. Beware of those spots, and be especially cautious when driving there. Stay alert even if you don't notice the police. If they are using radar, they will conceal themselves while selecting positions with clear and unobstructed views of oncoming traffic.

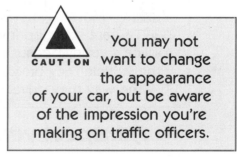

Make it a habit to stay within five miles of the speed limit to minimize the chance of attracting attention to your vehicle.

Finally, many police officers excuse minor violations and issue citations only for the most flagrant infractions. For example, citations are rare when driving less than 5mph over the limit.

3) Be mindful of appearances

The car you drive may have something to do with how often you are pulled over. Vehicles with an appearance of or reputation for speed catch an officer's eye before boxy beige sedans do. Cars that are customized, modified, souped up, slung low, or held together with rope and duct tape draw attention and suspicion.

CAUTION You may not want to change the appearance of your car, but be aware of the impression you're making on traffic officers.

4) Don't drink and drive

Perhaps no criminal violation is more socially charged or carries deeper repercussions than the charge of Driving Under the Influence (DUI), or, in

The easiest way to avoid a DUI charge? Don't drink and drive.

some states, Driving While Intoxicated or Driving While Impaired (DWI). It is difficult for anyone who has had "a few" drinks to know when not to get behind the wheel.

Traffic accidents

The investigation following a collision should be handled differently than a traffic stop, in which you are pulled over for a traffic violation. If the police determine, via the evidence at the scene, that you contributed to the accident or are responsible for it, you will receive a ticket.

Whether you are the cause or the victim of a collision, there are actions you need to take. Become familiar with them now, so they will come easily to mind following a collision.

- Carry pencil and paper in your car. Note color, make and plate number on the other car immediately following an accident, in case the other driver should leave the scene.

- Do not lose your temper or get into a shouting match with the other driver. Save any discussion until the police arrive.

- Take whatever steps are necessary to move cars and people out of danger, or to protect them from oncoming traffic.

- Attend to anyone who is injured, or get medical help. Make a note of the extent of injuries for future reference.

- Exchange information with the other drivers involved, or provide your information to the police: name, address, phone number, and information on driver's license, vehicle and insurance.

- Make your own inspection of the damage to both cars. Be especially observant of the damage to the other car to avoid being held responsible for unrelated damage.

- Do not make statements of guilt to the police. It is their job to determine the chain of events according to the evidence.

- Contact your insurance company as soon as possible for instructions on how to handle the aftermath of an accident.

- If the charges against you are serious, contact a lawyer before speaking to anyone else about the collision.

Avoiding a ticket once you are stopped

Despite your best efforts to avoid a traffic violation, statistics show you will get at least one ticket in the next four years. But a traffic stop doesn't have to end with a ticket. And a stop that seems to be heading toward arrest doesn't have to end in jail.

Here are some tips:

1) Be alert

As soon as you hear sirens or see flashing blue lights, be extra careful. If you are the target, further violations or suspicious moves will only increase your chances for getting a ticket—and possibly additional tickets for additional violations.

CAUTION Signal your intention to pull over so the officer recognizes that you responded appropriately. If you take too long, you may appear to be eluding the officer.

When you see the police car behind you with its emergency lights on, pull over quickly and safely. Pull well off the roadway to allow room for the officer to approach your window. On a busy road, look for a parking lot or similar location.

2) Stay in your car

As the officer approaches you, what should you do? Sit. Roll down your window. Keep your hands on the steering wheel in clear view. If it is nighttime, turn on your interior light.

If you leave your vehicle, the officer can interpret your actions as threatening, giving him or her probable cause to search you.

Do not get out of your car unless instructed to do so.

An officer has no right to search your car unless he or she has:

- Probable cause. For example, if the officer sees you or your passengers fumbling under the seat—or drugs, open alcohol containers, or weapons in the car—the officer has probable cause to search the vehicle.

- Your permission. If you refuse permission and the officer searches anyway, cooperate. You can fight the officer more successfully in court than in the street.

- A search warrant.

Keep your seat belt on as the officer approaches to avoid any question as to whether you were wearing it while operating the vehicle. Do not move suddenly, reach for items outside of the officer's view, or cause the officer concern for his or her own safety. Obey all instructions, so the officer sees you are not a threat.

3) Be prepared

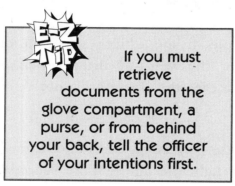

note

Keep your license, registration and, in most states, proof of insurance in an easy-to-reach place.

You may want to keep your registration on your person with your driver's license. The quicker you can produce these documents, the sooner the officer will put you at ease. Fumbling for them could lead to further inquiry and closer inspection.

When the officer asks for your license, remove it from its holder. Handing the officer your wallet, your credit cards, or your cash with your license may appear to be a bribe, which is illegal.

Wait silently for the officer to complete the routine of inspecting your driver's license and registration. Use the time to be observant: note the ticketing officer's name (on the uniform or your ticket). Is there a partner in the car? Who is driving? Note the time of day, the weather, the exact location, the glare of sun, lack of light, the directions you and the officer were traveling, any observers or passersby, and any vehicles that played a part in your violation. Any of these things may be important if you get a ticket and choose to fight it.

E-Z TIP

If you must retrieve documents from the glove compartment, a purse, or from behind your back, tell the officer of your intentions first.

What if you don't have your driver's license or registration on you? Say so. The officer may want to take your fingerprint. This is for your safety. Don't refuse; it is simply for identification purposes.

Whether or not you have the right documentation, the officer will probably run a computer check on your car. If you have any outstanding warrants or fines, the officer will learn about them.

4) Be cooperative

The officer is going to be very concerned about his or her own safety, particularly if the stop is at night or there are several passengers in the car. Cooperation is the key. Stay calm and do not raise suspicions.

In general, do not speak until spoken to, with one exception: Now is the time to state any legitimate reason for the driving that led to the stop. If, for example, there is a medical emergency, request that the fact be noted on the back of the officer's copy of the citation as proof that you offered this explanation when you were stopped.

Answer questions with a "yes" or a "no"; the less said the better. You've seen enough police shows to know you have the right to remain silent. Silence can't hurt you. Only words can.

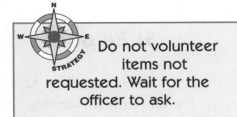

Do not volunteer items not requested. Wait for the officer to ask.

For instance:

- Never ask the officer why you were stopped, which can lead to your saying something that can be used against you in court.

- Never admit that you violated a law. ("I guess I was going a little too fast.")

- Never admit that you were inattentive or careless. ("I must have been too tired to pay attention to the signs.")

- Never say or do anything that will make you stand out from the dozens of violators the officer has stopped recently. Be forgettable. The less the officer remembers about you and the incident, the better.

• Never admit to "a couple of drinks." The officer probably won't believe you, and your admission to having consumed any alcohol may be used against you in court. If you have been drinking, "I prefer to remain silent" should be your answer to "How much have you been drinking?"

• Do not ask to see the results of the radar used to measure your speed.

• Never threaten the officer or lose your temper. Insist that your passengers cooperate too. Even if you are handcuffed, cooperate. If you believe the officer is out of line, you can fight back more successfully in court than you can on the street.

5) Be polite

When the officer says you are free to go, say "Thank you." If you've been let off with a warning, congratulations, you won. Pull back into traffic carefully, using proper signals and appropriate speed.

If you get a citation

citation

Chapter 2

If you get a citation

What you'll find in this chapter:

➠ Get familiar with court procedures

➠ Re-create the event for court

➠ Understand the penalties

➠ Know your options

➠ Using Motion For Continuance

If you get a citation, accept the ticket. Read the ticket. This will tell you exactly what you must disprove in court to win. Sign the ticket. This

note — Refusing a ticket is a crime.

acknowledges only that you received it, not that you are guilty of anything.

Later, carefully examine your citation. It specifies the fine and probably states the methods of payment. It will tell you the date by which you must pay the citation, if that's the option you choose. Keep this date in mind; if you lose your resolve to fight your ticket in court, you must pay by the stated date or risk losing your license and incurring costly reinstatement charges. It will also reflect on your driving record and could lead to greater penalties in future cases.

E-Z TIP

Any errors in these facts can be to your advantage when fighting the ticket, or can at least cast some doubt on the credibility of the ticketing police officer.

Your ticket cites the law you are accused of violating, which is vital when preparing your defense. Check to see that your ticket identifies your car by the correct plate number, state of registry, and make of vehicle.

Your citation may also direct you as to how to plead not guilty, and when and how to make such a plea. If you do not understand these instructions, call or visit the clerk of the court in the county where the citation was issued.

Get to know the clerk of the court

In many states the clerk of the court provides a wealth of information. In some courts the clerk not only records your ticket information but also whether you will pay the fine, attend traffic school, or plead not guilty. However, busy phones and long waiting lines are the rule in most traffic court clerks' offices. Be prepared when it's finally your turn:

- Have your ticket with you.

- Know your case or ticket number. (It's on your ticket.)

- Have pen and paper to record the date and time you called or visited the clerk's office, the name of the person you spoke to, and whatever information you received.

 Keep careful records. It's safest to assume that the court will keep no records at all. In fact, the first thing you should do is photocopy both sides of your ticket, so you have the information if the ticket is misplaced or must be turned in to the court.

The court clerk sends notices of important court dates to the address on your driver's license. If your address has changed, inform the clerk so you receive notice of when you must appear in court for your trial. Failure to inform the clerk of an address change is not considered a valid excuse for failing to appear in court.

If you forget your court date, call the clerk's office. Find out when your date is or was. If you missed it, go to the clerk's office immediately. Bring your ticket and cash. State your name and hand the clerk your ticket. When you appear before the judge, explain what happened honestly. The judge probably will excuse your failure to appear, but be prepared to pay an extra fine. If a warrant was issued, it will be set aside.

If you cannot pay the fine, the judge may give you additional time—usually 30 days—or may order community service work. Failure to appear, on the other hand, is a serious crime with a separate penalty—often

> *note*
>
> Don't forget your court date, and don't fail to appear because of a lack of funds to pay the citation.

the suspension of your license. If you are subsequently stopped while driving with a suspended license, your suspension period is extended. Eventually you can lose your license and be labeled a "habitual offender," all because of a failure to appear in court.

Re-creating the event for the court

As soon as possible after you get a ticket, write down all events that may be useful in court, including your conversation with the officer. Assume that the officer will do the same. Your court date may be delayed and memories fade. Your ability to recall small details could make a significant difference to the judge.

> **note**
> It may be necessary to return to the scene to observe anything you may have missed at the time of the citation.

If there were witnesses to the event, either in your car or on the street, get their names, addresses and phone numbers as soon as possible so you can contact them if you decide to go to court.

Depending on the reason for the ticket, you may want to return to the scene at the same time of day, under the same weather conditions, or with the same traffic patterns. Note distances, light conditions, density of traffic, poor visibility, absence of road signs, and road conditions. If diagrams, photographs, or drawings will help you explain the situation more clearly than words alone, they can be powerful tools in court. To be useful, they should be big enough to be seen easily.

Understand the penalties

To win in traffic court you must know and understand what you are up against. The judge can impose fines and costs up to the maximum allowed by law, order you to attend traffic school, suspend your license, or put you in jail or prison if the violation or your driving record is particularly bad.

Penalties vary according to violations. The more severe the violation, the more severe the penalty. Violations fit into three broad categories. From least to most severe they are:

- Infractions

- Misdemeanors

- Felonies

Every state categorizes traffic offenses differently. Infractions are usually civil offenses, while misdemeanors and felonies are criminal offenses. Prior offenses on your record can mean that an infraction, for example, will be upgraded to a misdemeanor. The best way to know how to categorize your offense is to check with the clerk's office in the county in which you were ticketed, review a driver's handbook from your state, or look up the code and section (as noted on your ticket) in the state statute.

You want to know:

- What is your violation?

- In which category does it belong?

- What are the maximum and minimum penalties?

The following are possible penalties:

1) Fines

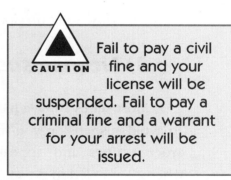

Fail to pay a civil fine and your license will be suspended. Fail to pay a criminal fine and a warrant for your arrest will be issued.

Fines, like most penalties, are based on the severity of the violation. Fines are treated differently depending on the type of case. If you are found guilty, the judge will announce your fine and when it must be paid. If you posted bail, the judge will consider the amount of bail that will be applied toward your fine. Rarely is a fine more than your posted bail. When you do pay your fine, request a receipt.

2) Points

Points on your driving record are a form of penalty that also track your violations. You get points only when you have been found guilty of a violation.

If you're found not guilty or the judge withholds adjudication or sentencing, neither the violation nor the points will appear on your record.

Points are assessed according to the violation. The more serious the violation, the more points; the more points, the greater your future penalties. Points also affect the cost and availability of insurance, and can eventually cause you to lose your license.

Again, check the state statutes, the clerk's office in traffic court, or a driver's handbook for an explanation of the point system in your state. Key questions you'll want to research include:

- How many points are assigned to your violation?

- How many points do you have currently?

- What is the limit for points in your state?

- How long do points remain on your record?

3) License suspension

Most states allow a judge to jail you for driving with a suspended license. To avoid suspension you must pay all ordered fines and appear in court when compelled to do so.

note — License suspension is a severe penalty.

You may also have your license suspended because you are a "habitual traffic offender." You are "habitual" when found guilty of a number of traffic violations within a short time period. For example, if you were found guilty of two DUIs and one felony within five years, you may be labeled a habitual traffic offender. States specify the applicable violations and time frame. Check your local statutes or your driver's license handbook, or call your local clerk's office.

4) Traffic school

Although traffic school is a penalty, it offers two benefits:

- It does not add more points to your record. (If you are close to the limit, this could make the difference between driving or walking to work.)

- It prevents the violation from going on your record.

 Whether you elect it or are sent by a judge, if you fail to attend traffic school, your license may be suspended or revoked, or you may be put in jail. In most states, the traffic school will not contact you. There may be limitations on how many times you can elect traffic school, so this option may not be available for future citations.

5) Jail

A jail sentence is imposed when your conduct has been too serious for the court to consider other alternatives. Jail may be imposed in addition to other penalties. You may request a stay of execution and enough time before you start serving your sentence to do whatever needs to be done before you comply with your penalty.

Your options

Now that you have an idea of the possible penalties, you must decide: Do you fight your ticket or simply pay it? These are your options:

1) Pay your ticket

By doing so you:

- admit your guilt

- pay the money

- have points assessed

- don't go to court

> **note** Some tickets, normally misdemeanors or felonies, require a court appearance. This may not be indicated on your ticket. Check with the clerk's office.

Your ticket usually indicates how much time you have to pay. If you don't have the money to pay the fine, write to the clerk or to the judge and request more time. Or offer to do community service work instead of paying the court costs or fines. Working for as little as $5 an hour is better than failing to pay the fine and losing your driving privilege.

2) Attend a diversionary program

Traffic school and other diversionary programs offer these benefits:

- no court appearance

- no points

You do usually pay costs, administrative fees, and fines, and not every traffic infraction offers the option of a diversionary program. Call the clerk's office to see if it is an option for you. If it is, find out exactly how to enroll. Remember, you must elect traffic school and other programs before you go to court.

If you choose traffic school rather than fight your ticket in court, you may also want to contact the state agency that regulates auto insurance to find out how your ticket may affect you, and how you can minimize the consequences.

3) Compliance

This means you must correct a deficiency. For example, if you receive a ticket for no proof of insurance, you must show proof of insurance at the clerk's office to keep your driving privileges. Compliance alone works only with certain violations.

The advantages of compliance:

- no fine or costs

- no points

- no court appearance

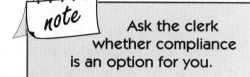

note

Ask the clerk whether compliance is an option for you.

- You may plead no contest (a plea that cannot be used against you)

4) Fight your ticket

You can fight your ticket whether it's a civil or criminal violation. Find out from the clerk's office how you get a hearing.

Why should you fight your ticket?

- to reduce your penalty

- to prove your innocence

The way to win is to go to court. In fact, it makes no difference whether you feel you are right or wrong. All that matters is whether the state can prove your guilt.

Court appearances

You must make a court appearance if you have been charged with a criminal violation and you elect a hearing. There are two ways to make an appearance:

- In person, which means either you or your attorney goes to court

- Appearance by Affidavit of Defense, which is a written statement of your defense. You must sign an Affidavit of Defense, have it notarized, and file it with the clerk's office. In addition, you will be required to post a bond. Use the Affidavit of Defense found in this guide, or ask the clerk's office how to obtain and file one.

DEFINITION

An *Affidavit of Defense* may be used in three situations:

- Non-resident status. You are not a resident of the county where the violation took place.

- Illness or absence. You cannot appear due to an extended illness or absence from the county where the violation took place.

- Special approval. You can get special approval from a hearing officer.

An Affidavit of Defense can also be used to present witness testimony, as explained in Chapter 5, Using Evidence.

Using a Motion for Continuance

If you or an important witness cannot appear on the scheduled date of the trial, you may submit a request to the court to reschedule the trial. This is usually done with a form called a Motion for Continuance, included in this guide. However, counties differ as to specific procedures for continuing a trial, and you should check with your clerk of court for specific information.

Most counties require you to notify the state of your request. Bear in mind that the state may be bringing witnesses and they, too, must be notified of the continuance. Obtain the granted continuance in writing from the clerk's office with the new date and time. If your continuance is denied, you must appear when scheduled.

Entering a plea

Chapter 3
Entering a plea

> **What you'll find in this chapter:**
> ⇒ Understand court terminology
> ⇒ Know your constitutional rights
> ⇒ Entering your plea
> ⇒ Understanding "no contest"
> ⇒ Plea negotiating

Before the date of your first appearance in court, prepare. Arriving late, flustered, disorganized, or distracted by other problems will irritate the judge or clerk and make the day more difficult.

Know where the court is ahead of time. The best plan includes a pre-court-date visit. Familiarize yourself with the building. Know the location of the traffic court, the courtroom and the bathroom. If you are driving, know where you can park, for how long, and for how much. If you are taking public transportation, know the closest stop or station and the schedule.

Find out if you can pay fines or court costs by check or credit card as well as in cash in the event that you must pay anything. Have your ticket (make a copy for yourself) ready for your court date. Expect your first appearance in court to take all day, although it could take ten minutes. Make appropriate arrangements for time away from work, for transportation, and for child care. Do not bring children to court.

E-Z TIP Whether you make a "trial run" beforehand or simply get to court earlier than necessary, watch the proceedings of other cases to get an idea of what you'll be doing when you stand before the judge.

Do not decide to fight the ticket in court until you review your driving record, available at the courthouse or driver's license bureau. The judge will certainly review it before making a decision. Also consider the alleged violation, the judge's reputation for handling similar cases, and the maximum penalty. Note: In some courts traffic officers are represented by counsel. By watching several hearings you will know whether this is true in your local court, and you can decide whether you should hire an attorney to represent you.

What is an arraignment?

An arraignment is your first appearance in court. Not every state has arraignments for traffic court. Your ticket will indicate whether you must attend an arraignment, in which case your court has a two-appearance system, the second appearance being your actual court appearance. In a one-appearance system you enter a plea and immediately attend a hearing. Either way, your first appearance includes the following steps:

- you are advised of your rights

- you are advised of the charge

- you enter a plea

Your constitutional rights

You have important constitutional rights. These include:

1) The right to a trial before a judge

Most traffic courts offer jury trials only for criminal violations, when the defendant may go to jail.

2) The right to cross-examine the witnesses who testify against you

This is your right to confrontation, or to face the state's witnesses and ask them questions.

3) The right to present witnesses on your own behalf

If you have witnesses, you will bring them to court the day of your hearing. Witnesses who support your position and are willing to testify strengthen your case.

4) The right to an attorney

note

A civil violation gives you no right to appointed counsel.

Although this guide is written for people who intend to represent themselves in traffic court, you can, in most states, hire an attorney to appear for you. If you cannot afford an attorney, one will be appointed (assigned to your case at no cost) only if you have been charged with a criminal violation and, therefore, risk going to jail.

5) The right to remain silent

Your right to avoid self-incrimination means that you cannot be forced to say anything that can be used against you. Also, you cannot be forced to be a witness against yourself.

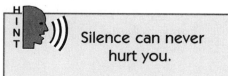

HINT

Silence can never hurt you.

6) The right to a speedy trial

You are entitled to a speedy trial if you have been charged with a criminal violation and have an arraignment before your trial. If your trial date is not set within a certain amount of time, your case will be dismissed. For example, a statute may require that you be brought to trial

If you request a later trial date (a motion for continuance), you waive your right to a speedy trial.

within 45 days of your arraignment. If your trial is set after the 45-day limit, your case is dismissed. If your violation is civil, you have no right to a speedy trial.

7) The right to be presumed innocent

You do not have to prove you are innocent, the state must prove you are guilty. If the state fails to prove your guilt, the judge must dismiss your case.

How to enter your plea

Enter your plea at the time of arraignment. If you don't have an arraignment, enter your plea at your hearing. When your name is called you should:

- stand up

- answer loudly

- answer clearly

In some courtrooms you come forward toward the bench (judge's desk) or a podium in front of it. In others you stand back unless the judge tells you to "approach the bench." Never lean on the podium. Always keep your hands at your sides.

Whether you are at a formal arraignment before a judge or stand informally before the clerk of the court, you must answer the charges with one of three pleas:

1) Guilty

There is a difference between automatically paying the fine to the clerk and accepting the points on your record, and pleading guilty and asking the judge not to enter a conviction on your driving record. The judge may or may not agree, but it is an important way to avoid points.

Ask the judge what the sentence will be if you plead guilty. Although not required to, most judges tell you what sentence to expect before imposing it. If you do not wish to subject yourself to the proposed penalties, you may plead not guilty and get a hearing.

The judge has your driving record and may ask about your driving history. Be honest. Never make false or misleading statements; they could lead to a harsher penalty.

> ⚠ **CAUTION** The judge has the sole authority to set the fine and court costs, up to the maximum allowed by law.

Since a guilty plea means that you admit to the charges, you also give up some of your constitutional rights. After you enter your guilty plea, the judge will sentence you.

2) Not guilty

 Whether you think you are not guilty or merely want to make the state prove its case, you should plead not guilty. This does not commit you to take the case to trial, but it is the essential first step and only way to get a trial.

Both the two-appearance system and the one-appearance system allow you to appear before a judge or magistrate for trial. Under both systems you inform the court that you want a trial by filing a written plea of not guilty with the clerk of court. This saves time, because you avoid going to court to enter your plea. To plead not guilty, the Notice of Appearance and Written Plea of Not Guilty form contained in this guide must be filed with the court clerk before the due date listed on the ticket, with a copy sent to the district or state attorney. Keep a copy for yourself.

Send your written plea (or any motion you file) to the court clerk by certified mail to prove delivery. If you hand-deliver it, have the clerk time-stamp your copy. If you mail your plea, contact the clerk by telephone to make sure it was received.

By pleading not guilty in writing you do not have to enter the plea personally. You will be notified in writing of your trial date, at which time you and your witnesses must appear. Note: you may request a trial by pleading not guilty, and then change your plea to guilty or no contest at trial. This can be done orally or in writing; a form to Request to Change Plea to No Contest is included in this guide.

3) No contest

DEFINITION

A plea of *no contest*, or *"nolo contendere,"* is essentially the same as a plea of guilty. It differs in that you are not admitting that you are guilty or that you committed the infraction. Instead, you are saying that while you do not admit the charges, it is not in your best interest to contest them through trial. This is a proper plea if, having watched other trials in your court, you see that a conviction is routinely entered against others who contest their cases. It is also the proper plea if you can't afford the time or the publicity associated with a trial.

DEFINITION

You may also ask the judge for permission to plead no contest with the right of explanation. You then explain any mitigating circumstances and ask the judge to *"withhold adjudication"* (or "suspend sentence" in some jurisdictions), which means there is no record of conviction and no points assessed.

If the judge agrees to this plea, be brief when explaining the circumstances. A lengthy story about why you are not guilty, coupled with a plea of no contest, may lead the judge to refuse your plea. Practice your explanation at home or with a friend. Keep it simple, honest and to the point.

As when pleading guilty, ask the judge what sentence would be imposed in consideration of the plea of no contest. Judges frequently impose lighter sentences for a plea of no contest than they would after a lengthy trial ending in a guilty finding.

One important advantage to a no-contest plea is that it cannot be used against you in a civil case. For example: You are in an accident and charged with criminal offenses to which you plead guilty. Later, if you are sued as a result of the same accident, those suing you can use your previous guilty plea to prove your liability. Had you pled no contest, it could not have been used against you.

Plea negotiating

DEFINITION

Before or during the trial, the state may try to convince you to "take a plea." When you *take a plea*, you plead guilty to your offense with the expectation of a reduction of your charge or lighter punishment.

You should not take a plea if your violation was an infraction. A reduction in charges won't mean anything. You can take traffic school instead.

There are four basic plea agreements:

- **Dismissal**. If you've been charged with more than one offense, some may be dismissed on the condition that you plead guilty to the remaining offenses.

- **Merger**. If you have two similar offenses, the state may consolidate them into one offense. You plead guilty to and face charges for only one offense.

- **Downgrading**. Your original offense is reduced to a less serious offense as long as you agree to plead guilty to this less serious offense.

- **Reduced sentence**. If you plead guilty, you will get a lighter sentence than you would get without a plea agreement. This may keep you out of jail; your sentence may even be reduced to a fine.

If you have been charged with a serious offense and you are in court because you believe you are innocent, taking a plea means giving up your right to a hearing and the possibility of having your case dismissed. Take a plea only if you welcome an opportunity to partially avoid the consequences of your traffic violation.

If you demanded a trial in order to make a deal with the state, now is the time to do it. You may be able to negotiate a reduction in your points or your fine.

The best way to get what you want is to persuade the state that there is something wrong with its case. Demonstrate that you have a winning case, without disclosing evidence that should be kept secret, and you may be offered a plea bargain.

Consider the following in deciding whether to take a plea:

- the chances of winning if you try your case

- the penalties that might result if you lose

- the benefits you would gain from entering a plea bargain

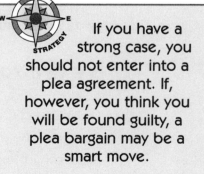

If you have a strong case, you should not enter into a plea agreement. If, however, you think you will be found guilty, a plea bargain may be a smart move.

How to prepare for trial

Chapter 4

How to prepare for trial

What you'll find in this chapter:

- ⇒ Researching laws and background
- ⇒ Identify the elements
- ⇒ Prepare yourself properly
- ⇒ Standard of Proof explained
- ⇒ How and when to subpoena witnesses

The three most important aspects of presenting a winning argument are preparation, preparation, and preparation.

Understand the law

A lawyer prepares for trial by researching the law allegedly violated. The statute you allegedly violated should be listed plainly on your citation. Go to a library and make several copies of the statute, including traffic law definitions. If your citation is for speeding, get a copy of the rules for maintaining and testing speed-measuring devices.

Definition:

Laws may be referred to as codes, ordinances, or statutes. In this guide they are referred to as statutes.

E-Z TIP: Find out where you can access the laws of your state, and ask for help in finding the law cited on your ticket.

Legal research is a good idea for anyone planning to fight a traffic ticket. Your public library probably has a law section, and law schools have extensive research libraries. Often a court will have a law library open to the public as well. Every clause of that law has to be proven for you to be found guilty.

Traffic laws list each of the necessary elements of the violation so that you may:

- determine if the state has proven each element of the alleged offense

- prepare your best defense, both factually and legally

- determine whether the correct statute was cited for the alleged offense

For your own preparation, outline and review the points the state must prove until you are thoroughly familiar with them. Determine what evidence you will need to cast doubt on the state's case. Should the state fail to prove each element of the statute, ask the judge for a "directed verdict" (dismissal of the case) by pointing out those elements unproven.

Identify the elements

A speeding statute, for example, may read: "No person shall operate a vehicle on a highway at a speed greater than 55 miles per hour." The state must prove:

- that you were the person behind the wheel

- that what you were doing was by definition driving

- that what was being operated was by definition a vehicle

- that where you were driving was by definition a highway

- that your speed was greater than 55 miles per hour, as measured in an approved manner

In another example, a traffic statute states: "The driver of a vehicle shall not follow another vehicle more closely than is reasonable and prudent, having due regard for the speed of such vehicles and the traffic upon and the condition of the highway." Here the state must prove:

- a vehicle was driven

- behind another vehicle

- more closely than is reasonable and prudent, considering the speed of the vehicles, other traffic and the condition of the roadway

The state may easily prove the first two elements. However, you may aggressively challenge the road, the weather, the speed of the other vehicles, the traffic on the roadway, and even introduce factors to justify the closeness of your vehicle.

Moreover, if the citation is issued after an accident, the operator of the front vehicle probably did not see the ramming vehicle before impact and could not testify how closely it trailed or how fast it was traveling. Because these facts comprise necessary elements, they each must be proven or the state has failed to prove its case.

If you've been charged with failing to observe a traffic sign, you may be able to prove that the sign was illegally installed. Although there are stringent state requirements for road signs, towns and cities often install the sign first and worry about the prerequisites later—if ever.

Sometimes just refreshing your knowledge of the rules of the road can help you win in traffic court. For example, in an unmarked intersection, the driver on the right has the right of way. Yet the police may, simply by overlooking that one rule, ticket the wrong driver.

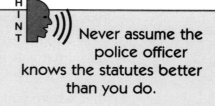

Never assume the police officer knows the statutes better than you do.

Some statutes can be violated several ways. If the law has several subparts, each constitutes a separate and distinct way the law can be violated. If the citation does not state which subpart you violated, move to dismiss the case. Tell the judge that the citation, as the charging document, violated your due process rights because the state must plainly inform you of the law you violated. Failure to place the correct statute, subpart and subsection on your citation does not adequately inform you as to what you have done wrong. Such a motion may win your case.

Now you see why outlining the violated statute and knowing what the state must prove are fundamental to preparing your defense.

What is the standard of proof?

The state must prove your guilt, but you must know what standard of proof the court requires. For a civil violation it is a simple preponderance of the evidence. There is a higher standard of proof for a criminal violation, because you risk a jail sentence: the state must prove you are guilty beyond reasonable doubt.

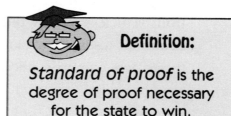

Definition:

Standard of proof is the degree of proof necessary for the state to win.

By law, the state has the burden of proof and must prove your guilt. But in real-world courtrooms, it tends to work the other way: Law officers are more convincing and more easily believed than defendants because they have more experience in the courtroom. They know how to state their case. They are not nervous. As a defendant, you must work harder to prove the officer wrong, and you must raise serious doubts about your guilt.

This is why research—both in the library and at the scene—can pay dividends. Diagrams and pictures may refute the police officer's story and tip the balance in your favor. Good research also helps you cross-examine and destroy testimony against you.

 You must create doubt. This is how you win in traffic court. When you create doubt in the judge's mind, the state has fallen short of meeting its burden of proof—and you win.

Prepare yourself

Why do most people lose in traffic court? Because they fail to consider seemingly small but significant factors. Your appearance will be the first impression you give. Make it a good one.

Dress conservatively. You don't want to stand out in this crowd. A suit is not required, but do wear a nice shirt or blouse with a pair of pants or a skirt. Do not wear jeans or shorts. Look neat and clean, with clothes

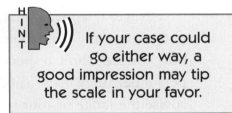

If your case could go either way, a good impression may tip the scale in your favor.

pressed and hair groomed. Gum, hats, gaudy jewelry, and toothpicks have no place in a courtroom.

Also, come into court with a pleasant attitude. Judges are not computers. The same violation can turn out differently for different defendants before the same judge.

The judge will be looking for:

- punctuality

- listening attentively

- not interrupting

- addressing the judge as "Your Honor" or "Judge"

- speaking loudly and clearly

- not speaking while others are talking

- not arguing with the judge

- being respectful of the police officers and witnesses against you

- sitting quietly until your case is called—without reading or other distractions that show disrespect to the court

Never appear haughty or indignant in the courtroom, no matter how you feel. Show respect to all court personnel; they have subtle ways to advise the judge of your rudeness.

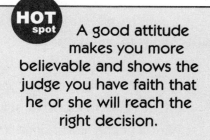

HOT spot A good attitude makes you more believable and shows the judge you have faith that he or she will reach the right decision.

Plan ahead

If you did not go to an arraignment, you may want to refer to Chapter 3, Entering A Plea, for some tips for your day in court. Briefly:

- Have your ticket with you on the date of your hearing.

- Review your version of the events several times before you go to court. Refer to the notes you made immediately after you got your ticket.

- Practice what you are going to say in front of a mirror or with a friend. Practice makes your argument more familiar and convincing, and will relax you on your court day.

There is a difference between practicing what you want to say and reading a written statement. Your words are more heartfelt and your point stronger if you speak naturally and make eye contact with the judge or witness. Rely on an outline of important points, rather than a script.

Subpoena witnesses

Even if your witness is your best friend, it's a good idea to issue a subpoena to ensure his or her attendance. Because subpoenas guarantee the appearance of your witnesses, they will think twice about missing your trial. The penalty for failing to appear may be contempt of court, a fine, or even a short stay in jail.

Definition:

A *subpoena* is an order to appear in court.

A subpoena also protects you if your witness fails to appear. The judge is more likely to allow a continuance if you did all you could to ensure that your witness would show.

To issue a subpoena you must:

- Obtain a subpoena form. Two are provided in this guide. The Subpoena for Trial requests the appearance of a person. The Subpoena for Trial (Duces Tecum) requests the appearance of a person possessing a specified document or item. Check with your clerk of court to see if another form is preferred. It may be provided, or you may be directed to a local office supply store.

- Fill out the subpoena, which is usually easy to complete. The clerk's office may help you if you have any questions. You will need the following information to complete the subpoena:

- name of the judge

- trial date and time

- address of the courthouse and the room number

- names of your witnesses

- home or work addresses of your witnesses

A subpoena must be "served," or officially delivered, by a court representative, process server or deputy sheriff, who must hand it to the witness. Certain requirements must be met for proper service. Check with the clerk's office for these requirements. Check your local Yellow Pages to locate a process server. There will be a nominal fee.

 You must also include a check for mileage, usually 25 to 30 cents per mile, with each subpoena. This is to reimburse the witness for the drive to the courthouse. It's safest to estimate the mileage generously.

Prepare your witnesses

Arm your witness with these six pointers:

1) Always be truthful.

2) Never change your story.

3) Never evade a proper question.

4) Keep answers short.

5) Never volunteer more information than is requested.

6) Never argue or take a hostile attitude.

Failure to comply with these tips will defeat the credibility and effectiveness of your witnesses.

Obtain information through discovery

The following should serve as background information, and is not recommended for the layperson. If you face criminal charges, you should seek the advice of counsel.

DEFINITION
In a criminal hearing, *discovery* is how the defense obtains any information the state has. If you are charged with a criminal violation, the law allows you to obtain a copy of all information relevant to your case. The state does not automatically issue discovery information; it must be requested. Copies of all correspondence should be retained.

The state, in response to such a request, may send:

- police reports

- witness statements

- qualifications of the officers who operated the radar or breath-testing equipment

- information on the accuracy of radar and breath-testing equipment

- laboratory results (i.e., blood alcohol levels)

Discovery will help win in traffic court in three ways:

1) The defense can see the state's case. If the state has a weak case, that can work to the defense's advantage, putting you more at ease or in a better position to plea bargain with the state.

2) The defense can read what the state's witnesses will say at trial. This aids in the preparation of the cross-examination.

3) The defense can check the accuracy of the officer's equipment. If the radar or breath-testing equipment used was not in compliance with regulations, the defense may be able to prevent the state from using that evidence.

> **HOT** spot It is important to reiterate here that this guide does not encourage a do-it-yourself defense against a criminal charge, which is when discovery is used. If you are charged with a criminal violation, seek the advice of counsel.

Motion to exclude witnesses

If more than one witness will testify for the state, you should request that they remain outside the courtroom when they are not testifying. Before the trial starts, simply make an oral motion to exclude witnesses from the courtroom—sometimes referred to as "invoking the rule."

Witnesses forget facts. If they hear other witnesses testify, they have a tendency to adopt what they hear as the truth. By "invoking the rule" you prevent the state's witnesses from adopting each others' stories to help prosecute you. Instead, you allow inconsistencies to surface because each witness has to testify solely on what he or she remembers, without any help from the others.

Your motion to exclude witnesses from the courtroom may also serve as an intimidation tactic against the state if the state has not had time to prepare its witnesses. With this motion, the state must worry whether the witnesses' stories will coincide.

Be aware that the state has the right to exclude your witnesses from the courtroom, too.

More on motions

You should be aware of several other motions that are useful in traffic court. One is the motion to dismiss, an oral request you make to dismiss the case against you. If the judge grants a motion to dismiss, you win in traffic court.

Make a motion to dismiss for lack of sufficient evidence if the police officer or a witness against you fails to appear in court. If your case involves an accident that the officer did not witness, and the other driver or witness does not appear, move to dismiss for lack of sufficient evidence. If the charges against you are serious, your motion may not be granted; the judge may want to reschedule the trial and give the state another chance to prosecute.

You must be tried in the correct court, or be within the court's jurisdiction. Similarly, if a local police officer (as opposed to a state police officer) gives you a ticket, be sure the offense you committed occurred within that officer's jurisdiction. If it did not, you may be able to use a motion to dismiss for lack of jurisdiction.

DEFINITION

For example, if you were given a ticket for speeding in Red County and the officer is from Green County, a motion to dismiss for lack of jurisdiction may succeed. You cannot be prosecuted in Green County, as Green County Court has no jurisdiction over you. Red County Court does, because your alleged offense occurred in Red County. *Jurisdiction* is where the offense was committed, not where you are ultimately stopped.

Renewal of motions

Any motion may be renewed throughout the trial. If the judge denied your motion initially, you may want to renew your motion if new information comes out during trial. You have nothing to lose by trying again.

Filing motions preserves your right to an appeal. If the trial judge denies your motion and you feel it was an error, your entire case could be reversed. It is up to you to use motions in your defense. The judge may not notice that the state has no jurisdiction or that the state failed to prove a *prima-facie* case. It is up to you to alert the judge to your defenses.

If the judge asks you a question about your motion—or about anything during the trial—answer as directly as you can. Start your answer with "Yes, Your Honor," or "No, Your Honor."

Using evidence

Chapter 5
Using evidence

What you'll find in this chapter:

➡ Tips on testifying

➡ Rules of evidence

➡ Types of evidence

➡ Examining and cross-examining witnesses

➡ Closing arguments

You win your case by destroying the state's case. You accomplish this by:

• presenting physical evidence or showing a lack of it

• your testimony and the testimony of your witnesses

• examining and cross-examining witnesses

• pointing out inconsistencies in the state's evidence

What is evidence?

Evidence that is tangible, such as a photograph, is called an exhibit; evidence that is verbal is called testimony.

Definition:
Evidence proves the truth or falsity of an issue.

1) Exhibits

Exhibits are documents, maps, photographs or other tangible items you offer as evidence in court. Before you enter any exhibit into evidence, you must first identify what your exhibit represents and establish that it's a fair and accurate reproduction of what it represents. You may be questioned about:

- Who created the exhibit or took the photograph?

- When was it created or taken?

- What is it supposed to show?

If the exhibit helps the judge better understand a point, it will be admitted. Convince the judge that your exhibit will do that.

2) Testimony

Testimony is verbal evidence provided by witnesses. The two keys judges look for in determining guilt or innocence are weight and credibility of evidence. Weight refers to the amount of evidence. Credibility refers to the strength of evidence.

The more witnesses you have, the greater your weight of evidence. The more independent your witnesses are, the greater your credibility of evidence.

Although strangers are more credible than friends, your passengers also make good witnesses since they are familiar with the facts. So are pedestrians who witnessed the event and support your position. That's why you need to get the names, addresses and phone numbers of potential witnesses immediately after the event—so you can contact them to testify later.

Review the testimony of each witness before the hearing to make sure the stories are consistent. If one witness' story varies from another's, don't use one of the witnesses. It's perfectly proper to discuss your case and the questions you will ask beforehand, and to know what your witnesses will say. In fact, no attorney would go into court without prepared witnesses.

On the other hand, make it clear to your witnesses that they must tell the truth even if they think it might do you harm. Instruct your witnesses to tell the prosecutor, when asked, that you told them always to tell the truth. You don't want the prosecution to imply that you coached witnesses to lie.

Affidavit of Defense

DEFINITION

Most states allow you to present the testimony of a witness in the form of an *affidavit*. This is a written and notarized document used when a witness will be out of state on the date of the trial, is ill, or has some other excusable reason for not attending the trial. To determine whether your state allows affidavits instead of live testimony, check with the clerk of court.

A valid affidavit:

- is typed or written legibly

- is signed in the presence of a notary public

- states why the witness cannot appear

- states what the witness saw and how the witness was able to make the observation

- addresses one or more of the elements in the case

This guide contains an Affidavit of Defense form that you can use for any witness who has a valid reason for not attending your trial. While it is useful, an affidavit does not have the power of personal testimony.

Should you testify?

You have the right to testify in your own defense, and you have the right to remain silent. Here are three factors to consider:

- You must be a good witness. If you think you could damage your case, don't testify.

- You will be subject to cross-examination. If you think the state might make you say something that will hurt your case, don't testify.

- Testifying strengthens your case. A judge is not supposed to look unfavorably on a defendant who doesn't testify, but if you don't testify, the judge may not believe you're innocent.

Rules of evidence

Not all evidence is admissible in a trial. When something is inadmissible at trial, it is considered objectionable. The judge decides whether proposed evidence is admissible or objectionable.

Formal rules determine what can be admitted as evidence in traffic court. But do not let this intimidate you; the rules are relaxed in this setting and you can depend on the judge for help. For example, if the state objects to evidence you are trying to admit, the judge will tell you what you must do to get it admitted.

Objections are made to prevent evidence from being admitted improperly. Objections are addressed only to the judge, who will "sustain" (uphold) or "overrule" (dismiss) the objection.

The quicker you object to a question being directed to a witness, the less likely improper and/or damaging evidence will be heard by the judge. When the judge sustains the objection, any improper evidence will be stricken from the record. Improper evidence not yet given will be blocked, as the witness will be prevented from answering. The state can also object to your improper evidence, as the rules apply to both sides.

Six examples of objectionable evidence:

1) Irrelevant evidence

Evidence must be relevant and prove one of the issues in your case. For example, if you're charged with speeding, evidence that you ran a red light is relevant. But evidence of your five prior parking tickets would be irrelevant; the parking tickets have nothing to do with speeding.

2) Hearsay

CAUTION To get your witnesses' statements admitted, have them testify as to what they saw or heard, rather than what someone else saw or heard.

Hearsay is an out-of-court statement offered to prove the truth of the matter asserted. Or, more simply, the witness is relating what someone else said as being true. Example: "Mrs. Smith told me the car was red." If the testimony is to prove the car was red, that statement is hearsay.

3) Conclusory statements

Only the judge may reach conclusions. The witnesses may only testify about facts. That is, they can tell their side of the story. A witness cannot say, "The defendant caused the accident." That is a conclusion.

4) Lack of foundation

Foundation questions are often required before you can admit certain evidence. These questions normally elicit background information. Without these preliminary questions, certain evidence would be irrelevant and, therefore, objectionable.

For example, if you are questioning an expert witness, your foundation questions would allow him to describe what makes him an expert. Only after his credentials are established can you ask him questions relating specifically to your case.

In another example, if a police officer is about to testify concerning the results of radar readings, and the state fails to first ask foundation questions establishing the officer's training and experience, you can object on the basis of "lack of foundation." The judge may agree to keep the radar results out of evidence.

5) Leading questions

Leading questions suggest an answer or tell a witness what to say. They can often be answered with a "yes" or "no."

Leading questions are not permissible on direct examination. If the state asks the officer, "You saw the defendant signal to turn left, didn't you?" you can object on the basis that it is a leading question. It suggests that the answer the state is looking for is "yes." A proper question would be, "What did you see?"

Leading questions are, however, permissible on cross-examination to impeach the credibility or veracity of witnesses.

6) The question was already asked and answered

The state may ask the officer or other witnesses the same question more than once. If the answer repeats unfavorable information about you, every reiteration drives it home in the judge's mind. When the state repeats a question it asked earlier, you may object. But be sure that the repeated question is trying to elicit the same previous answer. If the state is only trying to clarify what the witness said earlier, your objection will be overruled.

Insist upon proper evidence, but do not abuse objections. You will annoy the judge and perhaps lose your case.

Examining witnesses

Question your witnesses in a logical order. You can ask questions by subject, such as the weather or traffic conditions, or in chronological order, such as, "What happened after you walked to the parking lot?" and, "What happened next?"

When questioning your witnesses:

- Don't ask leading questions. You want facts established by your witnesses to bolster your case.

- Don't ask for hearsay.

- Don't ask for irrelevant details that will not help prove your innocence.

- Don't ask the important questions first. Build the evidence through testimony so that answers to your final questions leave the strongest impression of your innocence.

Cross-examining the state's witnesses

 When cross-examining you want to create doubt about the accuracy of the witnesses' testimony. Use leading questions to force a "yes" or "no" answer. Prepare your questions in advance so you obtain the answer you want. Finally, never ask a question if you don't already know the answer.

Control the cross-examination with leading questions. But beware that not all witnesses can be controlled easily. While most witnesses will passively agree to your leading questions, be prepared for an argumentative witness.

Your first questions should deal with points in agreement and lead to points in dispute, or those that will raise doubt about the state's case.

Example of a cross-examination:

Q. Is it true that at the distance you were from my car, your radar beam would be more than four lanes wide?

A. Yes.

Q. Were there at least three other cars in your view at the time you used your radar?

A. Yes.

Q. Is it possible that there might have been more than four cars?

A. Yes.

Q. At the distance you were from my car, doesn't your radar beam cover an area at least one lane to the right and one lane to the left of a target car?

A. Yes.

Q. Is it possible for your radar beam to pick up a target close to the car you intended to clock?

A. I aim at the car...

Q. Sir, the question is: Is it possible for your radar beam to pick up a target close to the car you intended to clock? Yes or no?

A. It's possible, but...

Q. Yes or no, sir.

A. Yes.

You can win your case by successfully attacking what a witness says. In traffic cases, witnesses frequently testify about events that occurred quickly and that they did not see directly. Congested traffic, weather conditions, distances, angles of sight,

> **HINT** Always attack the witness's ability to make accurate observations. Credibility involves truthfulness and accuracy of testimony.

and estimation of time are factors that limit a person's ability to testify accurately. You prove this inability through cross-examination.

Credibility fails when a witness cannot recall events. Memory fades with time. Because police officers issue so many citations, most find it difficult to remember specific facts about each case beyond what is in their notes.

In a case of running a red light, for example, the officer may have been far from the intersection and simultaneously observing the traffic, the traffic signal, the stop line or crosswalk, perhaps even his or her radar readings. This easily produces inaccurate testimony about when the vehicle entered the intersection and when the traffic light changed. Your cross-examination simply needs to establish that fact, citing factors like distance, distractions, angle, weather conditions, and the like.

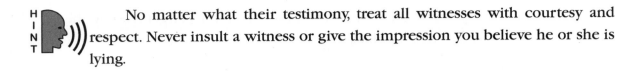

No matter what their testimony, treat all witnesses with courtesy and respect. Never insult a witness or give the impression you believe he or she is lying.

Closing arguments

The closing argument, or summation, is your final chance to convince the judge that your case should be dismissed. Briefly restate the evidence that supports your case. Your closing need not be lengthy, only persuasive.

Unlike testimony, a closing argument has no rules or set formula. You can argue your case creatively and in your own words, but keep it logical and accurate. Do not misquote a witness or fabricate facts not in evidence. You may look like a liar.

Prepare an outline of your closing argument and take additional notes during the trial. You'll better remember each witness's testimony and will be less likely to misstate what was said.

Your closing argument may, for example, recite the elements of the statute and how one or more of the elements remains unproven. Or you may tell why the state's proof was too weak for a conviction.

The state may have a closing argument also, but you should object if it is presented by the police officer, who would be unlawfully practicing law.

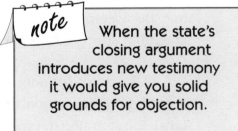

note When the state's closing argument introduces new testimony it would give you solid grounds for objection.

Driving under the influence

Chapter 6

Driving under the influence

What you'll find in this chapter:
⇒ When to get help from an attorney
⇒ What must be proved
⇒ Methods of testing blood alcohol level
⇒ Refusing a breath test
⇒ Understanding DUI penalties

DEFINITION Each year state legislatures make DUI laws tougher, making this area of the law extremely complex. The charge of *Driving Under the Influence* (DUI) or, in some states Driving While Intoxicated or *Driving While Impaired* (DWI) has such far-reaching ramifications that it should not be taken lightly.

The person presenting a DUI case must have a thorough working knowledge of this area of law and the facts of the case. This chapter is meant only to provide the facts concerning DUI charges.

 CAUTION An attorney should be consulted prior to making any decisions on the handling of a DUI or DWI case.

Proving DUI

The state must prove the elements of DUI beyond a reasonable doubt. Most states allow the police two ways to prove the charge of DUI:

- operating a motor vehicle while normal faculties are impaired by alcohol

- operating a motor vehicle with an unlawful blood-alcohol level

Operating while impaired

To prove that a driver's normal faculties were impaired by alcohol, the state must provide:

1) Proof that the driver was operating a motor vehicle

DEFINITION

Some states define *operating* in broad terms, such as being in a car on the side of the road with the keys in the ignition. Other states define the term more narrowly. In such states the driver in the above example might not be "operating a motor vehicle" because the car was stopped.

In determining whether a driver is operating a vehicle, a judge considers the following:

- identification of the defendant

- defendant's position in the vehicle

- location of the keys

- warm or cold engine

- operability of the vehicle

- location of the vehicle

- time and place of the offense

note The state must also prove the driver was intoxicated while driving or operating a motor vehicle. A driver who is able to prove he was sober at the time of the accident may get the case dismissed.

If, for example, a driver proves that he got into an accident, then went into a bar and had a few drinks, the state cannot convict him for DUI.

Some states limit DUI offenses to public areas. A driver in a private area—for example, a restaurant parking lot—can defend by claiming that he was operating a motor vehicle in a location that is not a public area. If the statute says the offense can occur anywhere, then private property is included.

2) Proof that normal faculties were impaired.

A person can appear to be intoxicated without consuming alcoholic beverages. An example is a person with a neuromuscular disease that makes him appear intoxicated. A doctor's letter would help a driver prove that an intoxicated appearance resulted from a medical condition, not from alcohol.

Definition:

Normal faculties are talking, walking, judging distances, etc. Sobriety tests are normally performed by the officer at the time of the violation, and become evidence that the driver appeared intoxicated.

The observations of the arresting officer or other witnesses can be challenged. A flushed face or red complexion could be the result of exposure to weather. Bloodshot eyes might be due to fatigue or crying. Balance problems could result from illness or apprehension. Nervousness could be the result of an inability to follow verbal directions. Testimony about slurred speech can be contradicted when the witness admits to never having spoken to the defendant before the encounter or arrest.

note

If the results of a chemical breath test or blood test are either unknown or rejected by the court, the state must prove impairment based solely on the observations and opinions of witnesses, which might include the arresting officer and back-up officers, video camera operators, personnel who administered the test, and bystanders. This testimony will include observations about the accused's driving and subsequent actions at the time of the arrest, including:

- deviant driving patterns, such as driving too fast or too slow, making wide turns and not maintaining a lane

- difficulty in pulling the vehicle over properly

- difficulty in locating license and registration

- problems in exiting the vehicle

- fluctuations in demeanor

- odor of alcohol on breath

CAUTION If a driver is advised of his right to remain silent and exercises that right, further questions must stop. However, any information volunteered by the driver after being advised of his rights may be used as evidence against him.

These observations can determine whether an arrest is made, and are significant in most DUI trials.

At the time of the accident or police stop, a driver may be asked to perform balancing and sobriety tests, but is not obligated to do so. He may be required to appear on video, but he cannot be made to say or do anything.

Other than refusing to submit to tests or answer questions, a driver charged with DUI should cooperate with police personnel. Statements admitting guilt and attempts to elicit compassion or understanding are not advised.

Operating with an unlawful BAC

DEFINITION

To prove an unlawful *blood-alcohol level* (also referred to as blood-alcohol count, or BAC), the state must prove that the level exceeded whatever standard is allowed by statute. This is usually .08 or .10, measured at the time the operator is driving.

Drivers in some states are given their choice of chemical tests. Blood and urine tests usually occur in hospitals. The urine test is most vulnerable to challenge in court, and the blood test is considered the most accurate.

> *note*
>
> A blood sample must be given after an accident involving death or serious bodily harm, and may be drawn forcibly from a driver.

Methods of testing

1) On-the-scene testing

The usual method for measuring blood-alcohol level is with a breath testing machine. A driver's license may be suspended for a year or more for refusal to take a test, even if the driver is later found not guilty.

2) Independent testing

In most states a driver charged with DUI has the right to an independent chemical test. If the state denies the request, the state may not be permitted to use the results of its own test, and the case can be dismissed.

A breath test must follow regulations or the result is invalid. Statutes dictate what state regulations are. Most states require that:

- the machine used for the testing be a particular type

- the machine used for testing be stored in a prescribed manner

- the device be periodically calibrated, inspected and maintained

- the machine be tested on the date the test was administered to the defendant

- the defendant be observed for a prescribed amount of time prior to the administration of the test

- the defendant be tested within a prescribed time frame following the stop

- the operator be properly trained and qualified

 If the state fails to prove any of these points, the judge may refuse to allow the test results. Therefore, defenses to the breath test can include:

- improper tests were administered

- the legal requirements were not complied with

- the operator was not qualified

- the test results showed no violation of the law

Breath-test results are universally accepted, subject to some specific limitations concerning observation periods, when the breath sample was taken, and deviation between several test results. Most courts even allow the state to attempt to establish the blood-alcohol level several hours prior to the test through a scientific principle known as retrograde extrapolation.

After a breath test

About two weeks following a breath test, the driver can make a written request for the results and information on how the analysis was made. This information is necessary in order to challenge a test in court.

Breath tests can be inaccurate for many reasons. A high reading may be caused by the reaction of chemicals in the equipment with chemicals in denture adhesive or lip ointment. A diabetic's breath may contain acetone, which produces a high reading. A bleeding gum condition or blood in the mouth caused in an accident will also elevate breath test results. Vapors of industrial chemicals on the person of the driver can affect the breath analysis.

> *note*
> Factors such as metabolism, body weight, and the time and nature of the last meal eaten can produce erroneous results.

note For conviction, the state must demonstrate that all legal requirements have been complied with. Through discovery and during trial, a defendant must inspect any documents the state submits to show the validity of the test results, the qualifications of the operator, and the inspection and maintenance reports. In any question of admissibility of evidence, it is in the defendant's best interest to object.

Two things can happen if the legal requirements have not been complied with. The test results can be found invalid and inadmissible, or they can be given less weight.

Refusing a breath test

Most states limit driving privileges after a DUI arrest. Depending on state law, driving privilege can be suspended for refusing a chemical test or simply for being arrested, with or without a conviction.

Refusing to submit to a breath or urine test will, in most states, result in suspension of driving privileges for six months to one year. The period could be longer for subsequent refusals. Laws of this type are not unconstitutional because driving is a privilege extended by the state government to its citizens. When signing the license, and thus agreeing to the terms of the privilege, every driver agrees to submit to a breath or urine test.

A person arrested for DUI may be better off refusing the breath test and accepting the license suspension, rather than submitting to the test and having a bad result made known to a jury. This is a judgment call that depends entirely on how much alcohol has been consumed over what period of time. If a license has been suspended due to such a refusal, most states have a program allowing the person to seek and attain a permit to drive on a limited basis. Generally referred to as a work permit, it allows driving to and from work, the grocery store, or for religious and medical reasons.

This guide strongly suggests retaining counsel to defend against a DUI charge.

Know the penalties for DUI

Almost every state has mandatory minimum penalties for DUI. This means the judge must impose at least a minimum sentence if the driver is found guilty or pleads no contest, and the judge can't impose a sentence greater than the statute's maximum. As with any traffic citation, community service may be substituted for DUI fines and court costs. The following are typical penalties:

- suspension of license for six months for a first conviction

- longer suspensions for more convictions

- probation for up to a year

- completion of a drug and alcohol program

- fines and court costs

- jail, usually mandatory if there are prior DUI convictions

Harsher penalties occur when:

- an accident causes substantial personal injury or death

- there are very high breath-test results

- there is a poor driving history

- driving was erratic or irresponsible

- there is misbehavior during a stop

Speeding and other traffic violations

7

Chapter 7

Speeding and other traffic violations

Speeding is the most common traffic rule infraction, and the one for which you are most likely to be cited. But in this chapter we also look at defenses for driving too slowly, driving with a suspended license, reckless driving, fleeing and eluding, parking tickets, and other traffic violations.

Driving too fast

Speeding is probably the most difficult violation to defend. The speed of a vehicle generally is determined by one of three methods:

- radar

- vascar

- racing

Each of the speed-measuring methods relies on the same basic principle: calculating speed by measuring the distance covered—over a monitored period of time.

These rules and regulations are in your state's traffic laws and are available from your secretary of state, the department of motor vehicles or the attorney general. You may also find these rules in a law library at your local courthouse, county library, or law school. The language in the rules may appear technical, but don't let this intimidate you.

To attack any speed-measuring method successfully, you must determine whether the police officer followed all written rules and regulations regarding the testing and use of the particular device.

Make copies of these regulations, and become familiar with them.

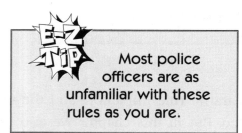

Most police officers are as unfamiliar with these rules as you are.

Underline such phrases as "the operator shall" or "each such device must," which indicate mandatory activities. The state's failure to adhere to those requirements can result in the judge refusing to allow the reading into evidence.

Elements of proof

The following are elements of proof for a speeding offense:

• **speed zone**

Violating a speed zone is known as violating a traffic control device. Examples of traffic control devices are speed limit signs, stop signs and traffic

If you can prove, for example, that a sign was blocked or knocked down, your case may be dismissed. The best way to prove that is to take a photograph of the sign.

markings. To be legal, these devices must be functional, in proper position, and legible enough to be seen.

- **posting of speed limit**

Check your local statutes to see if there is a requirement of adequate posting of speed-limit signs. Most states require that speed-limit signs be installed to give notice of the speed limit. Too few signs posted may prove you did not have proper notice of the speed limit.

note

Excessive speed is anything over the posted limit. Some states, however, have prima facie statutes. It is not necessarily unlawful to exceed the posted speed limit in those states; you can defend yourself by claiming that exceeding the speed limit was reasonable under the circumstances. Check your statutes to determine what the law is in your state.

If you do not want to use the defense techniques listed here, you may ask the judge for permission to plead no contest. For example, you may testify that the officer's opinion of your speed is inaccurate, but that you were exceeding the speed limit. Offer an explanation to justify your speed (do not use such excuses as your "speedometer was broken" or you were "just keeping up with the flow of traffic") and ask that a finding of fact be made that your speed was what you state it was. Then ask the judge to withhold an adjudication of guilt (thus avoiding the imposition of points) and assess reasonable court costs. The judge is likely to be impressed with your candor and enter the ruling you have requested.

How measuring devices work

Radar determines your speed by bouncing sonar waves off your vehicle and measuring the time it takes the vehicle to travel over a measured distance. Because it is complex, most states have stringent—often daily—testing requirements to ensure radar accuracy. Most modern units have internal accuracy checks to detect any problems.

The officer must also undertake a series of external checks specified in the regulations. These include checking the readouts, usually with a tuning fork, against at least one moving object. If tests are required before and after issuing citations, they

> **note** Written records must be maintained; compare them to the requirements to determine whether all necessary tests were made.

should be noted in the officer's log. If your state requires a written record of these tests and the daily log is deficient, object to any evidence that results from the use of radar.

DEFINITION

Vascar (Visual average speed computer device) determines speed by timing how long it takes a vehicle to travel a premeasured distance. As with radar, states usually have specific requirements for its use. The person who measured the distance must testify that the distance was measured properly. Periodic tests are required to determine if the device is properly calibrated. This must be done by technicians certified to conduct such tests.

DEFINITION

Pacing means the police vehicle maintains a constant position relative to your vehicle for a period of time, and determines your speed by measuring it against the speed of the police vehicle. Your best defense here is to question the accuracy of the police vehicle's speedometer. Most states require that police speedometers be tested every six months by a competent testing facility. A written certificate of accuracy must be presented in court; object if it is not.

Defenses to speed-measuring devices

- the operator's certificate was not produced in court

- the equipment certificate was not dated within six months of the ticket's issuance

- two log entries (one before and one after the ticket was issued) showing accuracy checks were not produced in court

- proof of speedometer calibration was not produced in court

Through discovery and during the trial, inspect any documents the state submits. If you are unsure about the admissibility of any of this evidence, it's better to object than allow improper evidence to be used against you.

If the state has not complied with the legal requirements, the evidence may be found invalid and inadmissible, or could be given less weight by the court. Either can be a successful defense.

Operator competency

Most states have specific competency requirements for the operators of speed-tracking devices. These requirements include:

- completion of a training course

- independent observation that the vehicle was speeding

- assurance that the ticket is based on a reading of a single vehicle

The more vehicles on the street, the less accurate the reading. Some doubt in the judge's mind gives you a successful defense. Cross-examine the officer to see if he mistakenly targeted your vehicle at someone else's speed. If the officer fails to meet the requirements, his or her reading will not be admitted and your case could be dismissed.

> **E-Z TIP** You have a valid defense if you can show that the street was crowded, and it was not necessarily your speed that was measured.

Driving too slow

You can get a ticket for going slower than the flow of traffic. Defenses for this offense are:

- your speed was safe for the conditions

- your speed was necessary for the safe operation of your car due to the type of cargo you were carrying

- your speed was due to an emergency condition

- your speed was due to dangerous road conditions

Driving with a suspended license

This is usually considered a criminal violation, not a civil violation. If you are caught driving under these conditions several times, you will be labeled a habitual offender, and the suspension can be permanent.

To prove you are serious about remedying your situation, never go to court to answer this charge without revalidating your license first, if at all possible. Explore any method your state allows that would enable you, even as a habitual offender, to appear in court with your driving privileges reinstated.

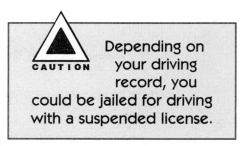

CAUTION Depending on your driving record, you could be jailed for driving with a suspended license.

To prove you were driving with a suspended license, the state must show:

- you were driving a motor vehicle

- you were driving while your driver's license was suspended or revoked

Defenses for driving with a suspended license:

- You never received notice of the suspension. If the state fails to prove that the proper notice was given, your case will be dismissed.

- Your suspension was improper. This could be due to a computer error, or the suspension could have expired and your license was reinstated. Bring proof of this to your trial and your case will be dismissed.

- You were not "operating a vehicle." Some states define "operating" as being in your car on the side of the road with the keys in the ignition; other states would not consider this "operating" your vehicle.

- You were not on a "public road." Check local statutes to determine whether the offense can occur anywhere, including private property (i.e., a restaurant parking lot), or whether the offense must occur in a public area.

Reckless driving

The state must prove two elements:

- you were driving a motor vehicle

- with a willful and wanton disregard for the safety of persons or property

Defenses for reckless driving are:

- no willful intent proven

- no intent to harm, just careless

- no clear proof, just the subjective opinion of the officer

- no accident occurred

- no witnesses

Fleeing and eluding

The state must prove two elements:

- you knew you had been directed to stop by the police

- you willfully failed to pull over and stop, or you did stop, but ran away

Defenses for fleeing and eluding are:

- you were not aware of the officer's presence

- you did not identify the person pulling you over as a law enforcement officer

- you did not see or hear the officer's order to stop

- you were unable to pull over due to dangers or hazards

Parking tickets

For most parking offenses, the state must prove all the following:

- a motor vehicle

- operated or owned by a person

- was illegally parked or stopped

- the vehicle had no special authorization to be there

Defenses to parking tickets are:

- The vehicle was in the care, custody or control of another person. You are responsible for payment of any parking violation on your car. However, if you did not have your car that day, you will have a successful defense. You must furnish to the police an affidavit stating the name, address and driver license number of the person who had control of your vehicle. This is also a valid defense if your car was stolen or in the control of another person who did not have permission to use your car.

- The ordinance was not offered into evidence. A state statute is recognized in court as valid. However, if your offense was a violation of a municipal ordinance, the prosecutor must offer a copy of the ordinance into evidence and ask the court to take judicial notice of the ordinance. If the prosecutor fails to do both, you should object based on the prosecutor's failure to prove the ordinance. Without proof of the ordinance, your case will be dismissed.

- Lack of proper marking. If you have a violation for parking next to or in front of an object, you may claim that the object was unmarked, improperly marked, or illegally marked, so it was impracticable or impossible to comply with the law. A photograph is your best evidence. You can use this defense with signs or markers that are obscure, illegible or inoperable.

- Emergency or authority. You may be able to claim that parking the vehicle was done to avoid a collision, damage or obstruction to other persons or vehicles. Alternatively, you can argue that the violation was done at the order of or with the consent of a law enforcement officer.

- The information on the ticket doesn't match your car or the time, date or place of the alleged offense. While there is a chance the judge will allow the officer to amend the ticket, it will probably be dismissed.

Defenses to parking in a handicapped parking zone are:

- You were chauffeuring a disabled person. A disabled person may be issued a parking permit entitling him or her to park in a handicapped space. You are allowed to park in these spaces for the purpose of loading or unloading this person. Bring the disabled person's permit to trial.

- The space was not properly designated and marked. You must show that the parking space was not prominently outlined with paint and was not posted with a permanent above-grade sign. Your best evidence is a photograph. Take it as soon as possible and bring it to court.

Other traffic defenses

- The description of the offense does not match the statute number. Generally, this defense won't work. The clerk's office always follows the statute number and the judge will allow the officer to amend the ticket.

- You do not own the car. This is another defense that won't work. If you were the operator, you will be charged with the offense.

- There was something wrong with the car. To prove this in court, you must bring your mechanic.

- You were sick. This is a good defense if, for example, you lost consciousness. You will have to prove in court that you were ill.

- **The officer didn't come to court. This is a good defense. Most of the time your case will be dismissed. However, if there are other witnesses, the case may still be tried.**

How to win after being found guilty

8

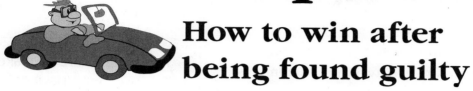

Chapter 8

How to win after being found guilty

The purpose of this guide is to help you win in traffic court, but if you are found guilty, you can minimize the consequences by making a special request to the judge. Consider:

Motion for reduction of penalty

This is an oral request to reduce imposed penalties. When arguing this motion, remind the judge of any mitigating circumstances. For instance, if you were found guilty of speeding, reminding the judge that you were rushing a sick passenger to the emergency room will likely result in a reduction of your penalty. Such a mitigating factor is used originally as a defense to the charge, but if you are found guilty, the same factor can be used in a motion to reduce the penalty.

Installment plans

If you must pay a fine, request permission to pay it in installments rather than in one lump sum. You'll be expected to demonstrate that a lump-sum payment would create a financial hardship for you. Do so by bringing a

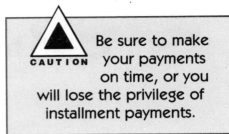

list of your monthly income and expenses. The judge is likely to grant your request.

Extension of time

If you get permission to pay in installments and then find you can't meet the payment schedule, go to court and ask the clerk for an extension of time. Your request should be made before you've fallen behind in payments, and before the next payment is due. The clerk will usually grant your request, especially if it is your first. If it is not your first request, you may have to go to the judge for an extension.

Limited driving privileges

If you lose your driving privileges, requesting a work permit may allow you to drive on a restricted basis, usually for employment or business purposes only. You must show that a suspension or revocation of your license will cause a serious hardship and interfere with your livelihood.

Rehabilitative programs

Programs such as drug or alcohol rehab are a common alternative to jail for DUI convictions. To persuade the judge that the rehabilitative alternative is warranted, bring a letter from your doctor stating that treatment will be more helpful to you than punishment.

Work release

You can request serving your jail time on weekends or at times that do not interfere with your opportunity to earn a living. This request is usually granted if you can prove you might otherwise lose your job.

Your right
to appeal

Chapter 9
Your right to appeal

The judge may render an opinion immediately after closing arguments are made. But the judge can take the case "under advisement" instead. This means a decision will come at some later date. The clerk's office can take two or three weeks to mail you the decision.

> **note**
> You may not be notified immediately when the judge's decision has been made.

If the judge's verdict is guilty and you want to appeal, you won't have much time after you've waited to receive a mailed notification; the time limit to appeal may be almost over. You may want to call the clerk's office about a week after your trial and ask if a decision has been rendered. If the answer is no, try again in a few days.

If the verdict is not guilty, you will get a refund of the bail you posted. Again, don't expect swift action on the part of the court; it may take months to receive your money.

Appeal

DEFINITION

An *appeal* is a request to have a higher court review the judge's decision. If you are unhappy with the outcome of your trial, you might consider appealing the decision.

There is one good reason to file an appeal: you want a remedy. An appeal may get you a new trial, which may lead to a reversal of your conviction. Also, while your appeal is pending, your sentence from the trial judge will be suspended.

There are three reasons why you should not file an appeal:

1) The cost of an appeal may exceed your initial penalty.

2) An appeal is complex. Consult an attorney to discuss your options. In fact, while it is not impossible to win in a court of appeal (or "appellate court") while representing yourself, it is not recommended.

3) The odds of winning an appeal are slim. If the facts as presented were accurate and there were no important errors or omissions in your court trial, the chances of convincing an appellate court to reverse the decision of the lower court are slim.

There are two ways to win an appeal:

• By proving that the evidence introduced at trial was insufficient to support the decision.

• By proving that the judge made an error that was prejudicial to your case. A prejudicial error is one that so affected your case that, had it not occurred, you would have been found not guilty or your case would have been dismissed.

There are rules to follow and forms to submit specific to your local court of appeal. There are also time limits to filing an appeal, which is why this guide does not recommend waiting until the traffic court mails you the judge's decision if you plan to appeal. Find out what the time limit is

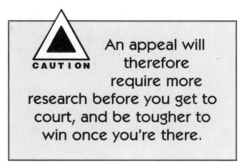

An appeal will therefore require more research before you get to court, and be tougher to win once you're there.

in your state and make the decision to appeal quickly. If you file too late, your appeal will be denied.

The decision is yours

Should you take your traffic ticket to court? Armed with the knowledge you've gathered since opening this book, you are the best person to make that decision.

Traffic court is, ostensibly, every driver's right. Unfortunately, from the traffic officer to the court clerk to the judge, the system has been designed to make it easiest simply to admit your guilt, pay your ticket, and get on with your life—whether you are guilty or not. It takes time, research, perseverance and commitment to take your ticket to traffic court, and there is no guarantee that you'll emerge victorious.

But going to court and insisting on your rights makes you an automatic winner in traffic court. Instead of following the crowd, you are exercising your rights. You are insisting that the traffic officer leave his or her post to attend a trial. You are forcing a judge to see an alternate point of view and consider the facts as you present them. You are refusing to donate your fine to the state's coffers. Win or lose, your experience in traffic court may encourage another person to do as you have done.

If enough drivers nationwide demand their legal rights, it will have a profound effect on the traffic enforcement system in the 21st century.

The forms in this guide

IN THE _____ COURT FOR _____ COUNTY
STATE OF _____

STATE OF _____,
                Plaintiff,

vs.

_____,
                Defendant.

Case : _____

NOTICE OF APPEARANCE AND WRITTEN PLEA OF NOT GUILTY

TO THE CLERK OF THE ABOVE STYLED COURT:

      YOU ARE HEREBY NOTIFIED that the undersigned is appearing pro se in the above-style cause, and you are hereby requested to furnish the undersigned with copies of all future motions, orders, etc., in this cause, particularly any notice for hearing or trial.

      FURTHERMORE the undersigned informs the Court that:

a. The above name Defendant is scheduled to be arraigned on

_____.

b. The Defendant hereby enters his plea of not guilty and requests a jury/non-jury trial and hereby waives formal arraignment and requests fifteen (15) days for filing appropriate defensive motions.

      I HEREBY CERTIFY that a copy of the foregoing has been furnished to the Office of the State Attorney, this _____ day of _____, _____.

By: _____

Address: _____

_____

Phone: _____

IN THE _____ COURT FOR _____ COUNTY
STATE OF _____

STATE OF _____,   Case no.: _____
                    Plaintiff,

vs.

_____,
                    Defendant.

MOTION FOR CONTINUANCE

       COMES NOW the Defendant, _____, appearing pro se, and pursuant to applicable rule of procedure moves this Court for the entry of an Order continuing the above-styled cause and for Defendant's cause would allege as follows:

       1. This cause is currently set for trial on _____ at _____.

       2. This is the first time this cause has been before the Court on the non-jury trial docket, and no previous continuance has been requested.

       3. Defendant respectfully requests this continuance due to the fact that _____

_____

_____

       4. This motion is made in good faith and is not meant to be dilatory in nature.

       WHEREFORE, Defendant, _____, prays this honorable Court enter and Order granting this Motion for Continuance made pursuant to the applicable rules of procedure.

       I HEREBY CERTIFY that a copy of the foregoing has been furnished to the Office of the State Attorney, this _____ day of _____, _____.

By: _____

Address: _____

_____

Phone: _____

IN THE _____ COURT FOR _____ COUNTY
STATE OF _____

STATE OF _____ ,
          Plaintiff,

vs.

_____ ,
          Defendant.

Case no.: _____

REQUEST TO CHANGE PLEA TO NO CONTEST

COMES NOW the Defendant, _____, appearing pro se, and notifies the Court of Defendant's Request to Change the previously entered plea of not guilty to that of no contest, and further would show unto the Court as follows:

1. Defendant is charged with _____.

2. Defendant hereby informs the Court of the desire to formally change the previously entered plea of not guilty to that of no contest, providing the Court either withholds adjudication of guilt or suspends sentence, or enters an Order in a manner which would not include a conviction of guilt for the offense, and further assess reasonable court costs to be paid within thirty (30) days of the date of the Order.

WHEREFORE, Defendant prays that the Court accept the Request for Change of Plea to No Contest, and resolve this case consistent with the requested contained herein.

I HEREBY CERTIFY that a copy of the foregoing has been furnished to the Office of the State Attorney, this _____, day of _____, _____.

By _____

Address: _____

_____

Phone: _____

IN THE COUNTY COURT FOR _____ COUNTY
STATE OF _____

_____,
       Plaintiff,

vs.

_____,
       Defendant.

_____

Case no.: _____

SUBPOENA FOR TRIAL

THE STATE OF _____:

TO _____:

      YOU ARE COMMANDED to appear before the Honorable _____,

Judge of the Court, at the _____ County Courthouse in the State

of _____, on _____, _____, at _____.m,

to testify in this action and to have with you at that time and place the following:

_____

_____

If you fail to appear, you may be in contempt of court.

      You are subpoenaed to appear by the undersigned, and unless excused from this subpoena by the undersigned, or the court, you shall respond on this subpoena as directed.

      DATED ON _____, _____.

Clerk of the Court

By _____
     Deputy Clerk

By _____

Address:_____

_____

Phone:_____

IN THE COUNTY COURT FOR _____ COUNTY
STATE OF _____

_____,
Plaintiff,

vs.   Case no.: _____

_____,
Defendant.

SUBPOENA FOR TRIAL (DUCES TECUM)

THE STATE OF _____:

TO _____:

        YOU ARE COMMANDED to appear before the Honorable _____,

Judge of the Court, at the _____ County Courthouse in the State

of _____, on _____,_____, at
_____.m,

to testify in this action and to have with you at that time and place the following:

_____

_____

If you fail to appear, you may be in contempt of court.

        You are subpoenaed to appear by the following attorneys, and unless excused from this subpoena by these attorneys, or the court, you shall respond on this subpoena as directed.

        DATED ON _____, _____.

                                        Clerk of the Court

                                        By _____
                                             Deputy Clerk

IN THE _____ COURT FOR COUNTY _____
STATE OF _____

STATE OF _____,
               Plaintiff,

    Case no.: _____

vs.

_____,
               Defendant.

_____

AFFIDAVIT OF DEFENSE

STATE OF _____)   SS

COUNTY OF _____)

       BEFORE ME, the undersigned authority, personally appeared

_____, who, being first duly sworn by me, deposes and says:

       1. The statements contained herein are made of my own personal knowledge.

       2. I cannot appear in court on _____ for the trial of _____ because _____

_____.

       3. I believe the defendant is not guilty of the alleged infraction because _____

_____

_____.

       4. I was able to make the observation because _____

_____.

FURTHER AFFIANT SAYETH NOT.

_____
               Affiant

       BEFORE ME, the undersigned notary public. personally appeared

_____, who is personally known to me, or produced identification in the form of a drivers' license, number _____, who read the foregoing document, acknowledged it to be true, and who did take an oath prior to signing this document.

       SWORN AND SUBSCRIBED to before me this _____ day of

_____, _____.

_____
             NOTARY PUBLIC

      State of _____

My Commission Expires:

Glossary of useful terms

Ac-Af

Accused

The person charged in a traffic case.

Acquittal

A finding of not guilty.

Adjudication

Judgment.

Adjudication withheld

A sentence is given but not expected to be served. Also called "suspending sentence."

Admissible evidence

Evidence that the judge allows to be considered in reaching the decision in the case.

Affidavit

A written statement made under oath.

Affidavit of Defense

A written statement saying the defendant has a good defense.

Al-Bl

Alleged

Claimed

Appeal

A request to a higher court to reconsider the decision of the trial court.

Appellate court

A court of review, as opposed to a trial court or court of first instance.

Appointed counsel

Attorney assigned to an indigent defendant at no cost.

Argument

The statements made in an effort to establish a defense.

Arraignment

The first appearance in court, when the charges are read and a plea is entered.

Bail

The amount of money needed to be released from jail. To "post bail" is to deliver the money required.

Bail bond

A guarantee that if the accused does not return to court, the person posting the bond will pay the bail money.

Blood-alcohol level

The quantity of alcohol in the blood.

Bu-Com

Burden of proof

The necessity of establishing guilt by the requisite degree.

Certified copy

A document that has been stamped with a seal indicating that it is a true and correct copy made by an authorized person.

Citation

A statement of the charge against a driver and a notice to appear. Technically, a release without bail. See "Traffic Ticket."

Civil traffic offense

Violation of a lesser traffic ordinance, as compared to a criminal traffic offense.

Clerk

Coordinator of the court.

Closing argument

The final statement to the judge in a hearing, when an attorney summarizes what has and has not been proven. Also called "summation."

Code

A compilation of laws.

Community service

A sentence requiring performance of work for the public good for a specific period of time.

Compliance

Obedience; correcting an equipment failure or lack of documentation to conform to traffic regulations.

Con-Cro

Conclusion

An objection that the witness is making a judgment rather than testifying as to what happened.

Confrontation

The right to face the witnesses against you in court.

Contempt of court

An intentional disregard of a court order. A showing of disrespect for the court.

Continuance

A postponement of the case to a later date.

Conviction

An adjudication of guilt.

Counsel

Attorney, or advice given by an attorney.

Court

The courthouse, the courtroom and/or the judicial officers.

Credibility

Believability.

Criminal traffic offense

Violation of a serious traffic law, as compared with a civil traffic offense.

Cross-examination

The questioning of witnesses by the opposing side.

D-

Defendant

See "Accused."

Defense

The case offered by the defendant in order to win.

Demonstrative evidence

Evidence other than the testimony of witnesses, such as photographs or drawings; also called "exhibits."

Directed verdict

Acquittal of the defendant because the state has failed to present a prima facie case.

Direct examination

The questioning of witnesses by the side calling the witnesses.

Discovery

The process of obtaining information from the state that relates to the case.

Dismissal

An order by the judge that terminates the case in favor of the defendant.

Diversionary program

A work or educational program designed for traffic offenders; see "Traffic School."

DUI

Driving Under the Influence of alcohol.

E-HA

Element

One of the parts of a traffic offense.

Elements of proof

The specific legal facts required to be proved in order to establish the guilt of the accused.

Evidence

Information that demonstrates the truth or falsehood of a point.

Exhibit

See "Demonstrative Evidence."

Felony

A crime that carries a prison sentence.

Finding of fact

A determination based on the evidence.

Foundation, lack of

An objection that a sufficient basis has not been laid to allow a witness to testify.

Guilty

A plea that admits the charge and allows the judge to sentence.

Habitual offender

Someone who repeatedly breaks the law, and consequently receives harsher sentencing.

HE-Ju

Hearing

A trial in which only the judge hears evidence and makes a finding.

Hearsay

An objection to testimony concerning what some person not present in the courtroom said.

Inadmissible evidence

Evidence that the judge does not allow to be considered.

Infraction

A noncriminal violation that is not punishable by incarceration, and that usually carries a fine.

Intent

The desire for a particular result.

Irrelevant

Immaterial; not applicable to the issue.

Judgment

The final decision of the court; also, the sentence of the court in criminal law.

Jurisdiction

The authority by which a court exercises power over a person, a case, or a geographical area.

Jury trial

A trial in which six to 12 of one's peers hear the evidence and decide the case.

L-No

Leading question

A question asked of a witness in a way that indicates how the witness should answer.

Mandatory

Containing a command; obligatory.

Merge

The absorption of one offense into another so that one of the offenses ceases to exist.

Misdemeanor

A crime that carries a maximum county jail penalty. Exception: petty misdemeanors carry only a fine.

Mitigating circumstances

Information the judge may consider in reducing the penalty for a traffic offense.

Motion

A formal request to the court.

Moving violation

Traffic violation for which points are added to the traffic record of the driver.

No contest

A plea that is treated the same as a guilty plea in allowing the judge to sentence. May not be used as an admission of guilt in a civil proceeding.

No-O

No contest with the right of explanation

A plea that does not acknowledge guilt but asks to present extenuating circumstances.

Nolo contendere

Latin for "I will not contest it." See "No contest."

Notarized

Certified by a notary public.

Not guilty

A plea that denies the charge and sets into motion the trial process.

Objection

A statement that one party does not want a statement by the other party to be considered by the court.

Offense

A violation or breach of the traffic law.

Ordinance

Laws enacted by the community, as opposed to statutes, which are enacted by the state.

Overrule

To reject or disallow; the opposite of "sustain."

P-Prim

Pacing

Measuring speed by matching the speed of the patrol car with the other vehicle.

Penalty

Punishment, usually a fine.

Penalty assessment

A sum of money added to a fine.

Plea

The answer given by the defendant to the charge.

Plea bargain

A deal made between the prosecution and the defendant to reduce the charge or fine. A procedure for settling cases before trial.

Point count

Numbers given to each conviction of a moving violation. Added together they can result in license suspension.

Prejudicial error

A court's error that could have had an effect on the outcome of a trial; it may be grounds for an appeal and new trial.

Prima facie

Latin for "on the face of it." Refers to evidence good and sufficient on its face to get a conviction for the state, unless the defendant can produce evidence to the contrary.

Pri-Pub

Prior

Refers to a previous conviction of a specific crime that increases the penalty for a new offense.

Process server

Someone authorized by law to deliver, and thus notify, another of some action or proceeding.

Pro se

To represent yourself in a court proceeding.

Probable cause

Facts and observations that would lead a reasonable person to believe that the accused has committed a crime.

Proceeding

A court case.

Proof

The result or effect of evidence.

Prosecution

A proceeding instituted by the state against someone who has violated a traffic law.

Prosecutor

Attorney representing the people, i.e., state, county or city.

Public defender

Attorney assigned to represent those without money in criminal cases when jail is a possible outcome. Also called "appointed counsel."

R-Si

Radar

A means of determining speed by bouncing electronic signals off a moving vehicle and measuring how fast they return.

Reinstatement of license

When the period of suspension or revocation of one's driving privilege has passed and one can legally drive again.

Revocation

Termination of a licensee's privilege to drive a motor vehicle.

Search

Seeking out, by a police officer, of something illegal on one's person or in one's motor vehicle.

Search warrant

A written order issued by a judge directing a police officer to search for and seize property in connection with a crime.

Section

The numbered subparts of a law.

Self-incrimination

When a person says or does something before or during a trial that implicates that person in a crime.

Sentence

The imposed punishment announced by the judge following conviction.

Simple preponderance of evidence

A standard of proof in civil cases in which the weight or credibility of the state's evidence is greater than the evidence for the defendant.

Sp-Sus

Speed measurements

The results of radar or other devices designed to measure the speed of moving vehicles.

Standard of proof

The degree of proof required for the state to obtain a conviction, such as "beyond a reasonable doubt."

State

The body of people of any state who are considered wronged by a violation of the traffic law.

Statute

A law established and enacted by a state legislature.

Stay of execution

Temporary postponement of punishment to allow the perpetrator time to prepare.

Subpoena

A court order requiring the appearance in court of the person receiving the order.

Subpoena duces tecum

A court order for the production in court of material things, such as documents or papers.

Suspension

The temporary withdrawal of a licensee's privilege to drive a motor vehicle.

Sus-T

Suspended sentence

Sentencing given formally but not served. See "Adjudication withheld."

Sustain

To grant or allow; the opposite of "overrule."

Testimony

Oral evidence given by a witness.

Traffic clerk

An administrator who sends traffic cases into the courtroom, accepts bail and fine money and may be able to set court appearances and grant extensions for payment of fines.

Traffic court

The court that considers traffic cases in an informal fashion without the strictness and technicalities of major court litigation.

Traffic school

An education program that allows ticketed drivers to avoid a conviction or additional points.

Traffic ticket

A document issued by all law enforcement agencies to operators of motor vehicles for traffic law violations. See "Citation."

Trial

The formal examination of a case by the court.

V-W

Verdict

The formal decision made by a jury or judge.

Violation

See "Offense."

Waive

To give up or relinquish.

Witness

Someone who testifies as to what he or she has seen, heard or experienced.

Resources

••• Online Resources •••

◆ **Advocates for Highway and Auto Safety**

http://www.saferoads.org

◆ **AAA Foundation for Traffic Safety**

http://www.aaafts.org

◆ **American Association of Motor Vehicle Administrators (AAMVA).**

http://www.aamva.net

◆ **American Driver and Traffic Safety Education Association (ADTSEA)**

http://adtsea.iup.edu/adtsea

◆ **C.A.N.D.I.D. (Citizens Against Drug Impaired Drivers)**

http://www.candid.org

◆ **Drivers.Com**

http://drivers.com

◆ **Federal Highway Administration, U.S. Department of Transportation Office of Highway Safety**

http://www.ohs.fhwa.dot.gov

◆ **Insurance Institute for Highway Safety**

http://www.hwysafety.org

◆ **International Association for Chemical Testing**

http://www.iactonline.org

◆ **Mobile Scanner & Radar Detector Laws in the United States**

http://www.afn.org/~afn09444/scanlaws

◆ **National Highway Traffic Safety Administration**

http://www.nhtsa.dot.gov

◆ **National Motorists Association**

http://www.motorists.com

◆ **Radio Association Defending Airwave Rights, Inc. (RADAR)**

   http://www.radar.org

◆ **United States Departments of Transportation U.S. Department of Transportation**

   http://www.dot.gov/internet/usadots.html

◆ **Transport Accident Commission (TAC)**

   http://www.tac.vic.gov.au

◆ **WWW Speedtrap Registry, Inc.**

   http://www.speedtrap.com

◆ **Yahoo! Business and Economy > Companies > Automotive > Driving Schools**

   http://dir.yahoo.com/Business_and_Economy/Companies/Automotive/Driving_Schools/Traffic_Schools/

◆ **Yahoo! Recreation > Automotive > Driving > Safety**

   http://dir.yahoo.com/Recreation/Automotive/Driving/Safety/Organizations

◆ **Yahoo! Society and Culture > Crime > Crimes > Drunk Driving**

   http://dir.yahoo.com/Society_and_Culture/Crime/Crimes/Drunk_Driving/Organizations

◆ **ZapMe! netspace - Electives - Drivers Education -**

http://www.zapme.com/net/class/electives/electives_drivers.htm let.org/lpm/lpdiv/estate.html

••• Legal Search Engines •••

◆ **All Law**

http://www.alllaw.com

◆ **American Law Sources On Line**

http://www.lawsource.com/also/searchfm.htm

◆ **Catalaw**

http://www.catalaw.com

◆ **FindLaw**

URL: http://www.findlaw.com

◆ **Hieros Gamos**

http://www.hg.org/hg.html

◆ **InternetOracle**

http://www.internetoracle.com/legal.htm

◆ **LawAid**

http://www.lawaid.com/search.html

◆ **LawCrawler**

http://www.lawcrawler.com

◆ **LawEngine, The**

http://www.fastsearch.com/law

◆ **LawRunner**

http://www.lawrunner.com

◆ **'Lectric Law Library**™

http://www.lectlaw.com

◆ **Legal Search Engines**

http://www.dreamscape.com/frankvad/search.legal.html

◆ **LEXIS/NEXIS Communications Center**

http://www.lexis-nexis.com/lncc/general/search.html

◆ **Meta-Index for U.S. Legal Research**

http://gsulaw.gsu.edu/metaindex

◆ **Seamless Website, The**

http://seamless.com

◆ **USALaw**

http://www.usalaw.com/linksrch.cfm

◆ **WestLaw**

http://westdoc.com (Registered users only. Fee paid service.)

••• State Bar Associations •••

ALABAMA

Alabama State Bar
415 Dexter Avenue
Montgomery, AL 36104
mailing address:
PO Box 671
Montgomery, AL 36101
(334) 269-1515

http://www.alabar.org

ALASKA

Alaska Bar Association
510 L Street No. 602
Anchorage, AK 99501
mailing address:
PO Box 100279
Anchorage, AK 99510

http://www.alaskabar.org

ARIZONA

State Bar of Arizona
111 West Monroe
Phoenix, AZ 85003-1742
(602) 252-4804

http://www.azbar.org

ARKANSAS

Arkansas Bar Association
400 West Markham
Little Rock, AR 72201
(501) 375-4605

http://www.arkbar.org

CALIFORNIA

State Bar of California
555 Franklin Street
San Francisco, CA 94102
(415) 561-8200

http://www.calbar.org

Alameda County Bar
Association

http://www.acbanet.org

COLORADO

Colorado Bar Association
No. 950, 1900 Grant Street
Denver, CO 80203
(303) 860-1115

http://www.cobar.org

CONNECTICUT

Connecticut Bar Association
101 Corporate Place
Rocky Hill, CT 06067-1894
(203) 721-0025

http://www.ctbar.org

DELAWARE

Delaware State Bar Association
1225 King Street, 10th floor
Wilmington, DE 19801
(302) 658-5279
(302) 658-5278 (lawyer referral
service)

http://www.dsba.org

DISTRICT OF COLUMBIA

District of Columbia Bar
1250 H Street, NW, 6th Floor
Washington, DC 20005
(202) 737-4700

Bar Association of the District
of Columbia
1819 H Street, NW, 12th floor
Washington, DC 20006-3690
(202) 223-6600

http://www.badc.org

FLORIDA
The Florida Bar
The Florida Bar Center
650 Apalachee Parkway
Tallahassee, FL 32399-2300
(850) 561-5600
http://www.flabar.org

GEORGIA
State Bar of Georgia
800 The Hurt Building
50 Hurt Plaza
Atlanta, GA 30303
(404) 527-8700
http://www.gabar.org

HAWAII
Hawaii State Bar Association
1136 Union Mall
Penthouse 1
Honolulu, HI 96813
(808) 537-1868
http://www.hsba.org

IDAHO
Idaho State Bar
PO Box 895
Boise, ID 83701
(208) 334-4500
http://www2.state.id.us/isb

ILLINOIS
Illinois State Bar Association
424 South Second Street
Springfield, IL 62701
(217) 525-1760
http://www.illinoisbar.org

INDIANA
Indiana State Bar Association
230 East Ohio Street
Indianapolis, IN 46204
(317) 639-5465
http://www.ai.org/isba

IOWA
Iowa State Bar Association
521 East Locust
Des Moines, IA 50309
(515) 243-3179
http://www.iowabar.org

KANSAS
Kansas Bar Association
1200 Harrison Street
Topeka, KS 66612-1806
(785) 234-5696
http://www.ksbar.org

KENTUCKY
Kentucky Bar Association
514 West Main Street
Frankfort, KY 40601-1883
(502) 564-3795
http://www.kybar.org

LOUISIANA
Louisiana State Bar Association
601 St. Charles Avenue
New Orleans, LA 70130
(504) 566-1600
http://www.lsba.org

MAINE

Maine State Bar Association
124 State Street
PO Box 788
Augusta, ME 04330
(207) 622-7523

http://www.mainebar.org

MARYLAND

Maryland State Bar Association
520 West Fayette Street
Baltimore, MD 21201
(301) 685-7878

http://www.msba.org/msba

MASSACHUSETTS

Massachusetts Bar Association
20 West Street
Boston, MA 02111
(617) 542-3602
(617) 542-9103 (lawyer referral
service)

http://www.massbar.org

MICHIGAN

State Bar of Michigan
306 Townsend Street
Lansing, MI 48933-2083
(517) 372-9030

http://www.michbar.org

MINNESOTA

Minnesota State Bar Association
514 Nicollet Mall
Minneapolis, MN 55402
(612) 333-1183

http://www.mnbar.org

MISSISSIPPI

The Mississippi Bar
643 No. State Street
Jackson, Mississippi 39202
(601) 948-4471

http://www.msbar.org

MISSOURI

The Missouri Bar
P.O. Box 119, 326 Monroe
Jefferson City, Missouri 65102
(314) 635-4128

http://www.mobar.org

MONTANA

State Bar of Montana
46 North Main
PO Box 577
Helena, MT 59624
(406) 442-7660

http://www.montanabar.org

NEBRASKA

Nebraska State Bar Association
635 South 14th Street, 2nd floor
Lincoln, NE 68508
(402) 475-7091

http://www.nebar.com

NEVADA

State Bar of Nevada
201 Las Vegas Blvd.
Las Vegas, NV 89101
(702) 382-2200

http://www.nvbar.org

NEW HAMPSHIRE

New Hampshire Bar
Association
112 Pleasant Street
Concord, NH 03301
(603) 224-6942

http://www.nhbar.org

NEW JERSEY

New Jersey State Bar
Association
One Constitution Square
New Brunswick, NJ 08901-1500
(908) 249-5000

NEW MEXICO

State Bar of New Mexico
5121 Masthead N.E.
Albuquerque, NM 87125
mailing address:
PO Box 25883
Albuquerque, NM 87125
(505) 843-6132

http://www.nmbar.org

NEW YORK

New York State Bar Association
One Elk Street
Albany, NY 12207
(518) 463-3200

http://www.nysba.org

NORTH CAROLINA

North Carolina State Bar
208 Fayetteville Street Mall
Raleigh, NC 27601
mailing address:
PO Box 25908
Raleigh, NC 27611
(919) 828-4620

North Carolina Bar Association
1312 Annapolis Drive
Raleigh, NC 27608
mailing address:
PO Box 3688
Cary, NC 27519-3688
(919) 677-0561

http://www.ncbar.org

NORTH DAKOTA

State Bar Association of North
Dakota
515 1/2 East Broadway, suite 101
Bismarck, ND 58501
mailing address:
PO Box 2136
Bismarck, ND 58502
(701) 255-1404

OHIO

Ohio State Bar Association
1700 Lake Shore Drive
Columbus, OH 43204
mailing address:
PO Box 16562
Columbus, OH 43216-6562
(614) 487-2050

http://www.ohiobar.org

OKLAHOMA

Oklahoma Bar Association
1901 North Lincoln
Oklahoma City, OK 73105
(405) 524-2365

http://www.okbar.org

OREGON

Oregon State Bar
5200 S.W. Meadows Road
PO Box 1689
Lake Oswego, OR 97035-0889
(503) 620-0222
http://www.osbar.org

PENNSYLVANIA

Pennsylvania Bar Association
100 South Street
PO Box 186
Harrisburg, PA 17108
(717) 238-6715
http://www.pabar.org

Pennsylvania Bar Institute
http://www.pbi.org

PUERTO RICO

Puerto Rico Bar Association
PO Box 1900
San Juan, Puerto Rico 00903
(787) 721-3358

RHODE ISLAND

Rhode Island Bar Association
115 Cedar Street
Providence, RI 02903
(401) 421-5740
http://www.ribar.org

SOUTH CAROLINA

South Carolina Bar
950 Taylor Street
PO Box 608
Columbia, SC 29202
(803) 799-6653
http://www.scbar.org

SOUTH DAKOTA

State Bar of South Dakota
222 East Capitol
Pierre, SD 57501
(605) 224-7554
http://www.sdbar.org

TENNESSEE

Tennessee Bar Assn
3622 West End Avenue
Nashville, TN 37205
(615) 383-7421
http://www.tba.org

TEXAS

State Bar of Texas
1414 Colorado
PO Box 12487
Austin, TX 78711
(512) 463-1463
http://www.texasbar.com/start.htm

UTAH

Utah State Bar
645 South 200 East, Suite 310
Salt Lake City, UT 84111
(801) 531-9077
http://www.utahbar.org

VERMONT

Vermont Bar Association
PO Box 100
Montpelier, VT 05601
(802) 223-2020
http://www.vtbar.org

VIRGINIA

Virginia State Bar
707 East Main Street, suite 1500
Richmond, VA 23219-0501
(804) 775-0500

Virginia Bar Association
701 East Franklin St., Suite 1120
Richmond, VA 23219
(804) 644-0041
http://www.vbar.org

VIRGIN ISLANDS

Virgin Islands Bar Association
P.O. Box 4108
Christiansted, Virgin Islands
00822
(340) 778-7497

WASHINGTON

Washington State Bar
Association
500 Westin Street
2001 Sixth Avenue
Seattle, WA 98121-2599
(206) 727-8200
http://www.wsba.org

WEST VIRGINIA

West Virginia State Bar
2006 Kanawha Blvd. East
Charleston, WV 25311
(304) 558-2456
http://www.wvbar.org

West Virginia Bar Association
904 Security Building
100 Capitol Street
Charleston, WV 25301
(304) 342-1474

WISCONSIN

State Bar of Wisconsin
402 West Wilson Street
Madison, WI 53703
(608) 257-3838
http://www.wisbar.org/
home.htm

WYOMING

Wyoming State Bar
500 Randall Avenue
Cheyenne, WY 82001
PO Box 109
Cheyenne, WY 82003
(307) 632-9061
http://www.wyomingbar.org

How to save on attorney fees

How to save on attorney fees

Millions of Americans know they need legal protection, whether it's to get agreements in writing, protect themselves from lawsuits, or document business transactions. But too often these basic but important legal matters are neglected because of something else millions of Americans know: legal services are expensive.

They don't have to be. In response to the demand for affordable legal protection and services, there are now specialized clinics that process simple documents. Paralegals help people prepare legal claims on a freelance basis. People find they can handle their own legal affairs with do-it-yourself legal guides and kits. Indeed, this book is a part of this growing trend.

When are these alternatives to a lawyer appropriate? If you hire an attorney, how can you make sure you're getting good advice for a reasonable fee? Most importantly, do you know how to lower your legal expenses?

When there is no alternative

Make no mistake: serious legal matters require a lawyer. The tips in this book can help you reduce your legal fees, but there is no alternative to good professional legal services in certain circumstances:

- when you are charged with a felony, you are a repeat offender, or jail is possible

- when a substantial amount of money or property is at stake in a lawsuit

- when you are a party in an adversarial divorce or custody case

- when you are an alien facing deportation

- when you are the plaintiff in a personal injury suit that involves large sums of money

- when you're involved in very important transactions

Are you sure you want to take it to court?

Consider the following questions before you pursue legal action:

What are your financial resources?

Money buys experienced attorneys, and experience wins over first-year lawyers and public defenders. Even with a strong case, you may save money by not going to court. Yes, people win millions in court. But for every big winner there are ten plaintiffs who either lose or win so little that litigation wasn't worth their effort.

Do you have the time and energy for a trial?

Courts are overbooked, and by the time your case is heard your initial zeal may have grown cold. If you can, make a reasonable settlement out of court. On personal matters, like a divorce or custody case, consider the emotional toll on all parties. Any legal case will affect you in some way. You will need time away from work. A newsworthy case may bring press coverage. Your loved ones, too, may face publicity. There is usually good reason to settle most cases quickly, quietly, and economically.

How can you settle disputes without litigation?

Consider *mediation*. In mediation, each party pays half the mediator's fee and, together, they attempt to work out a compromise informally. *Binding arbitration* is another alternative. For a small fee, a trained specialist serves as judge, hears both sides, and hands down a ruling that both parties have agreed to accept.

So you need an attorney

Having done your best to avoid litigation, if you still find yourself headed for court, you will need an attorney. To get the right attorney at a reasonable cost, be guided by these four questions:

What type of case is it?

You don't seek a foot doctor for a toothache. Find an attorney experienced in your type of legal problem. If you can get recommendations from clients who have recently won similar cases, do so.

Where will the trial be held?

You want a lawyer familiar with that court system and one who knows the court personnel and the local protocol—which can vary from one locality to another.

Should you hire a large or small firm?

Hiring a senior partner at a large and prestigious law firm sounds reassuring, but chances are the actual work will be handled by associates—at high rates. Small firms may give your case more attention but, with fewer resources, take longer to get the work done.

What can you afford?

Hire an attorney you can afford, of course, but know what a fee quote includes. High fees may reflect a firm's luxurious offices, high-paid staff and unmonitored expenses, while low estimates may mean "unexpected" costs later. Ask for a written estimate of all costs and anticipated expenses.

How to find a good lawyer

Whether you need an attorney quickly or you're simply open to future possibilities, here are seven nontraditional methods for finding your lawyer:

1) **Word of mouth**: Successful lawyers develop reputations. Your friends, business associates and other professionals are potential referral sources. But beware of hiring a friend. Keep the client-attorney relationship strictly business.

2) **Directories**: The Yellow Pages and the Martin-Hubbell Lawyer Directory (in your local library) can help you locate a lawyer with the right education, background and expertise for your case.

3) **Databases**: A paralegal should be able to run a quick computer search of local attorneys for you using the Westlaw or Lexis database.

4) **State bar associations**: Bar associations are listed in phone books. Along with lawyer referrals, your bar association can direct you to low-cost legal clinics or specialists in your area.

5) **Law schools**: Did you know that a legal clinic run by a law school gives law students hands-on experience? This may fit your legal needs. A third-year law student loaded with enthusiasm and a little experience might fill the bill quite inexpensively—or even for free.

6) **Advertisements**: Ads are a lawyer's business card. If a "TV attorney" seems to have a good track record with your kind of case, why not call? Just don't be swayed by the glamour of a high-profile attorney.

7) **Your own ad**: A small ad describing the qualifications and legal expertise you're seeking, placed in a local bar association journal, may get you just the lead you need.

How to hire and work with your attorney

No matter how you hear about an attorney, you must interview him or her in person. Call the office during business hours and ask to speak to the attorney directly. Then explain your case briefly and mention how you obtained the attorney's name. If the attorney sounds interested and knowledgeable, arrange for a visit.

The ten-point visit

1) Note the address. This is a good indication of the rates to expect.

2) Note the condition of the offices. File-laden desks and poorly maintained work space may indicate a poorly run firm.

3) Look for up-to-date computer equipment and an adequate complement of support personnel.

4) Note the appearance of the attorney. How will he or she impress a judge or jury?

5) Is the attorney attentive? Does the attorney take notes, ask questions, follow up on points you've mentioned?

6) Ask what schools he or she has graduated from, and feel free to check credentials with the state bar association.

7) Does the attorney have a good track record with your type of case?

8) Does he or she explain legal terms to you in plain English?

9) Are the firm's costs reasonable?

10) Will the attorney provide references?

Hiring the attorney

Having chosen your attorney, make sure all the terms are agreeable. Send letters to any other attorneys you have interviewed, thanking them for their time and interest in your case and explaining that you have retained another attorney's services.

Request a letter from your new attorney outlining your retainer agreement. The letter should list all fees you will be responsible for as well as the billing arrangement. Did you arrange to pay in installments? This should be noted in your retainer agreement.

Controlling legal costs

Legal fees and expenses can get out of control easily, but the client who is willing to put in the effort can keep legal costs manageable. Work out a budget with your attorney. Create a timeline for your case. Estimate the costs involved in each step.

Legal fees can be straightforward. Some lawyers charge a fixed rate for a specific project. Others charge contingency fees (they collect a percentage of your recovery, usually 35-50 percent if you win and nothing if you lose). But most attorneys prefer to bill by the hour. Expenses can run the gamut, with one hourly charge for taking depositions and another for making copies.

Have your attorney give you a list of charges for services rendered and an itemized monthly bill. The bill should explain the service performed, who performed the work, when the service was provided, how long it took, and how the service benefits your case.

Ample opportunity abounds in legal billing for dishonesty and greed. There is also plenty of opportunity for knowledgeable clients to cut their bills significantly if they know what to look for. Asking the right questions and setting limits on fees is smart and can save you a bundle. Don't be afraid to question legal bills. It's your case and your money!

When the bill arrives

- **Retainer fees**: You should already have a written retainer agreement. Ideally, the retainer fee applies toward case costs, and your agreement puts that in writing. Protect yourself by escrowing the retainer fee until the case has been handled to your satisfaction.

- **Office visit charges**: Track your case and all documents, correspondence, and bills. Diary all dates, deadlines and questions you want to ask your attorney during your next office visit. This keeps expensive office visits focused and productive, with more accomplished in less time. If your attorney charges less for phone consultations than office visits, reserve visits for those tasks that must be done in person.

- **Phone bills**: This is where itemized bills are essential. Who made the call, who was spoken to, what was discussed, when was the call made, and how long did it last? Question any charges that seem unnecessary or excessive (over 60 minutes).

- **Administrative costs**: Your case may involve hundreds, if not thousands, of documents: motions, affidavits, depositions, interrogatories, bills, memoranda, and letters. Are they all necessary? Understand your attorney's case strategy before paying for an endless stream of costly documents.

- **Associate and paralegal fees**: Note in your retainer agreement which staff people will have access to your file. Then you'll have an informed and efficient staff working on your case, and you'll recognize their names on your bill. Of course, your attorney should handle the important part of your case, but less costly paralegals or associates may handle routine matters more economically. Note: Some firms expect their associates to meet a quota of billable hours, although the time spent is not always warranted. Review your bill. Does the time spent make sense for the document in question? Are several staff involved in matters that should be handled by one person? Don't be afraid to ask questions. And withhold payment until you have satisfactory answers.

- **Court stenographer fees**: Depositions and court hearings require costly transcripts and stenographers. This means added expenses. Keep an eye on these costs.

- **Copying charges**: Your retainer fee should limit the number of copies made of your complete file. This is in your legal interest, because multiple files mean multiple chances others may access your confidential information. It is also in your financial interest, because copying costs can be astronomical.

- **Fax costs**: As with the phone and copier, the fax can easily run up costs. Set a limit.

- **Postage charges**: Be aware of how much it costs to send a legal document overnight, or a registered letter. Offer to pick up or deliver expensive items when it makes sense.

- **Filing fees**: Make it clear to your attorney that you want to minimize the number of court filings in your case. Watch your bill and question any filing that seems unnecessary.

- **Document production fee**: Turning over documents to your opponent is mandatory and expensive. If you're faced with reproducing boxes of documents, consider having the job done by a commercial firm rather than your attorney's office.

- **Research and investigations**: Pay only for photographs that can be used in court. Can you hire a photographer at a lower rate than what your attorney charges? Reserve that right in your retainer agreement. Database research can also be extensive and expensive; if your attorney uses Westlaw or Nexis, set limits on the research you will pay for.

- **Expert witnesses**: Question your attorney if you are expected to pay for more than a reasonable number of expert witnesses. Limit the number to what is essential to your case.

- **Technology costs**: Avoid videos, tape recordings, and graphics if you can use old-fashioned diagrams to illustrate your case.

- **Travel expenses**: Travel expenses for those connected to your case can be quite costly unless you set a maximum budget. Check all travel-related items on your bill, and make sure they are appropriate. Always question why the travel is necessary before you agree to pay for it.

- **Appeals costs**: Losing a case often means an appeal, but weigh the costs involved before you make that decision. If money is at stake, do a cost-benefit analysis to see if an appeal is financially justified.

- **Monetary damages**: Your attorney should be able to help you estimate the total damages you will have to pay if you lose a civil case. Always consider settling out of court rather than proceeding to trial when the trial costs will be high.

- **Surprise costs**: Surprise costs are so routine they're predictable. The judge may impose unexpected court orders on one or both sides, or the opposition will file an unexpected motion that increases your legal costs. Budget a few thousand dollars over what you estimate your case will cost. It usually is needed.

- **Padded expenses**: Assume your costs and expenses are legitimate. But some firms do inflate expenses—office supplies, database searches, copying, postage, phone bills—to bolster their bottom line. Request copies of bills your law firm receives from support services. If you are not the only client represented on a bill, determine those charges related to your case.

Keeping it legal without a lawyer

The best way to save legal costs is to avoid legal problems. There are hundreds of ways to decrease your chances of lawsuits and other nasty legal encounters. Most simply involve a little common sense. You can also use your own initiative to find and use the variety of self-help legal aid available to consumers.

11 situations in which you may not need a lawyer

1) **No-fault divorce**: Married couples with no children, minimal property, and no demands for alimony can take advantage of divorce mediation services. A lawyer should review your divorce agreement before you sign it, but you will have saved a fortune in attorney fees. A marital or family counselor may save a seemingly doomed marriage, or help both parties move beyond anger to a calm settlement. Either way, counseling can save you money.

2) **Wills**: Do-it-yourself wills and living trusts are ideal for people with estates of less than $600,000. Even if an attorney reviews your final documents, a will kit allows you to read the documents, ponder your bequests, fill out sample forms, and discuss your wishes with your family at your leisure, without a lawyer's meter running.

3) **Incorporating**: Incorporating a small business can be done by any business owner. Your state government office provides the forms and instructions necessary. A visit to your state office will probably be

necessary to perform a business name check. A fee of $100-$200 is usually charged for processing your Articles of Incorporation. The rest is paperwork: filling out forms correctly; holding regular, official meetings; and maintaining accurate records.

4) **Routine business transactions**: Copyrights, for example, can be applied for by asking the U.S. Copyright Office for the appropriate forms and brochures. The same is true of the U.S. Patent and Trademark Office. If your business does a great deal of document preparation and research, hire a certified paralegal rather than paying an attorney's rates. Consider mediation or binding arbitration rather than going to court for a business dispute. Hire a human resources/benefits administrator to head off disputes concerning discrimination or other employee charges.

5) **Repairing bad credit**: When money matters get out of hand, attorneys and bankruptcy should not be your first solution. Contact a credit counseling organization that will help you work out manageable payment plans so that everyone wins. It can also help you learn to manage your money better. A good company to start with is the Consumer Credit Counseling Service, 1-800-388-2227.

6) **Small Claims Court**: For legal grievances amounting to a few thousand dollars in damages, represent yourself in Small Claims Court. There is a small filing fee, forms to fill out, and several court visits necessary. If you can collect evidence, state your case in a clear and logical presentation, and come across as neat, respectful and sincere, you can succeed in Small Claims Court.

7) **Traffic Court**: Like Small Claims Court, Traffic Court may show more compassion to a defendant appearing without an attorney. If you are ticketed for a minor offense and want to take it to court, you will be asked to plead guilty or not guilty. If you plead guilty, you can ask for leniency in sentencing by presenting mitigating circumstances. Bring any witnesses who can support your story, and remember that presentation (some would call it acting ability) is as important as fact.

8) **Residential zoning petition**: If a homeowner wants to open a home business, build an addition, or make other changes that may affect his or her neighborhood, town approval is required. But you don't need a lawyer to fill out a zoning variance application, turn it in, and present your story at a public hearing. Getting local support before the hearing is the best way to assure a positive vote; contact as many neighbors as possible to reassure them that your plans won't adversely affect them or the neighborhood.

9) **Government benefit applications**: Applying for veterans' or unemployment benefits may be daunting, but the process doesn't require legal help. Apply for either immediately upon becoming eligible. Note: If your former employer contests your application for unemployment benefits and you have to defend yourself at a hearing, you may want to consider hiring an attorney.

10) **Receiving government files**: The Freedom of Information Act gives every American the right to receive copies of government information about him or her. Write a letter to the appropriate state or federal agency, noting the precise information you want. List each document in a separate paragraph. Mention the Freedom of Information Act, and state that you will pay any expenses. Close with your signature and the address the documents should be sent to. An approved request may take six months to arrive. If it is refused on the grounds that the information is classified or violates another's privacy, send a letter of appeal explaining why the released information would not endanger anyone. Enlist the support of your local state or federal representative, if possible, to smooth the approval process.

11) **Citizenship**: Arriving in the United States to work and become a citizen is a process tangled in bureaucratic red tape, but it requires more perseverance than legal assistance. Immigrants can learn how to obtain a "Green Card," under what circumstances they can work, and what the requirements of citizenship are by contacting the Immigration Services or reading a good self-help book.

Save more; it's E-Z

When it comes to saving attorneys' fees, Made E-Z Products is the consumer's best friend. America's largest publisher of self-help legal products offers legally valid forms for virtually every situation. E-Z Legal Kits and the Made E-Z Guides which cover legal topics include all necessary forms and a simple-to-follow manual of instructions or a layman's book. Made E-Z Books are a library of forms and documents for everyday business and personal needs. Made E-Z Software provides those same forms on disk and CD for customized documents at the touch of the keyboard.

You can add to your legal savvy and your ability to protect yourself, your loved ones, your business and your property with a range of self-help legal titles available through Made E-Z Products.

Whatever you need to know, we've made it E-Z!

Informative text and forms you can fill out on-screen.* From personal to business, legal to leisure—we've made it E-Z!

PERSONAL & FAMILY

For all your family's needs, we have titles that will help keep you organized and guide you through most every aspect of your personal life.

BUSINESS

Whether you're starting from scratch with a home business or you just want to keep your corporate records in shape, we've got the programs for you.

  (INCORPORATION, CORPORATE RECORD KEEPING, ACCOUNTING)

   (YOUR PROFITABLE HOME BUSINESS, OWNING A FRANCHISE, WEBSITE MARKETING)

* Not all topics include forms   ss 1999.r2

FEDERAL & STATE
Labor Law Posters

The Poster 15 Million Businesses Must Have This Year!

All businesses must display federal labor laws at each location, or risk fines and penalties of up to $7,000!
And changes in September and October of 1997 made all previous Federal Labor Law Posters obsolete;
so make sure you're in compliance—use ours!

State	Item#	State	Item#	State	Item#
Alabama	83801	Louisiana	83818	Ohio	83835
Alaska	83802	Maine	83819	Oklahoma	83836
Arizona	83803	Maryland	83820	Oregon	83837
Arkansas	83804	Massachusetts	83821	Pennsylvania	83838
California	83805	Michigan	83822	Rhode Island	83839
Colorado	83806	Minnesota	83823	South Carolina	83840
Connecticut	83807	Mississippi	83824	South Dakota not available	
Delaware	83808	Missouri	83825	Tennessee	83842
Florida	83809	Montana	83826	Texas	83843
Georgia	83810	Nebraska	83827	Utah	83844
Hawaii	83811	Nevada	83828	Vermont	83845
Idaho	83812	New Hampshire	83829	Virginia	83846
Illinois	83813	New Jersey	83830	Washington	83847
Indiana	83814	New Mexico	83831	Washington, D.C.	83848
Iowa	83815	New York	83832	West Virginia	83849
Kansas	83816	North Carolina	83833	Wisconsin	83850
Kentucky	83817	North Dakota	83834	Wyoming	83851

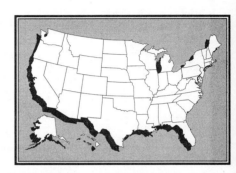

State Labor Law Compliance Poster
Avoid up to $10,000 in fines by posting the
required State Labor Law Poster available from
Made E-Z Products.

$29.95

Federal Labor Law Poster
This colorful, durable 17³/₄" x 24" poster is in
full federal compliance and includes:

- The NEW Fair Labor Standards Act Effective
  October 1, 1996
  (New Minimum Wage Act)

- The Family & Medical Leave Act of 1993*

- The Occupational Safety and Health
  Protection Act of 1970

- The Equal Opportunity Act

- The Employee Polygraph Protection Act

* Businesses with fewer than 50 employees should display reverse
side of poster, which excludes this act.

$11.99
Stock No. LP001

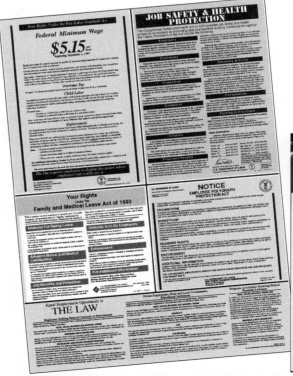

ss1999.r2

See the order form in this guide to order yours today!

By the book...

	Item#	Qty.	Price Ea.‡
★ **E♦Z Legal Kits**			
Bankruptcy	K100		$23.95
Incorporation	K101		$23.95
Divorce	K102		$29.95
Credit Repair	K103		$21.95
Living Trust	K105		$21.95
Living Will	K106		$23.95
Last Will & Testament	K107		$18.95
Buying/Selling Your Home	K111		$21.95
Employment Law	K112		$21.95
Collecting Child Support	K115		$21.95
Limited Liability Company	K116		$21.95
★ **Made E♦Z Software**			
Accounting Made E-Z	SW1207		$29.95
Asset Protection Made E-Z	SW1157		$29.95
Bankruptcy Made E-Z	SW1154		$29.95
Best Career Oppportunities Made E-Z	SW1216		$29.95
Brain-Buster Crossword Puzzles	SW1223		$29.95
Brain-Buster Jigsaw Puzzles	SW1222		$29.95
Business Startups Made E-Z	SW1192		$29.95
Buying/Selling Your Home Made E-Z	SW1213		$29.95
Car Buying Made E-Z	SW1146		$29.95
Corporate Record Keeping Made E-Z	SW1159		$29.95
Credit Repair Made E-Z	SW1153		$29.95
Divorce Law Made E-Z	SW1182		$29.95
Everyday Law Made E-Z	SW1185		$29.95
Everyday Legal Forms & Agreements	SW1186		$29.95
Incorporation Made E-Z	SW1176		$29.95
Last Wills Made E-Z	SW1177		$29.95
Living Trusts Made E-Z	SW1178		$29.95
Offshore Investing Made E-Z	SW1218		$29.95
Owning a Franchise Made E-Z	SW1202		$29.95
Touring Florence, Italy Made E-Z	SW1220		$29.95
Touring London, England Made E-Z	SW1221		$29.95
Vital Record Keeping Made E-Z	SW1160		$29.95
Website Marketing Made E-Z	SW1203		$29.95
Your Profitable Home Business	SW1204		$29.95
★ **Made E♦Z Guides**			
Bankruptcy Made E-Z	G200		$17.95
Incorporation Made E-Z	G201		$17.95
Divorce Law Made E-Z	G202		$17.95
Credit Repair Made E-Z	G203		$17.95
Living Trusts Made E-Z	G205		$17.95
Living Wills Made E-Z	G206		$17.95
Last Wills Made E-Z	G207		$17.95
Small Claims Court Made E-Z	G209		$17.95
Traffic Court Made E-Z	G210		$17.95
Buying/Selling Your Home Made E-Z	G211		$17.95
Employment Law Made E-Z	G212		$17.95
Collecting Child Support Made E-Z	G215		$17.95
Limited Liability Companies Made E-Z	G216		$17.95
Partnerships Made E-Z	G218		$17.95
Solving IRS Problems Made E-Z	G219		$17.95
Asset Protection Secrets Made E-Z	G220		$17.95
Immigration Made E-Z	G223		$17.95
Buying/Selling a Business Made E-Z	G223		$17.95
★ **Made E♦Z Books**			
Managing Employees Made E-Z	BK308		$29.95
Corporate Record Keeping Made E-Z	BK310		$29.95
Vital Record Keeping Made E-Z	BK312		$29.95
Business Forms Made E-Z	BK313		$29.95
Collecting Unpaid Bills Made E-Z	BK309		$29.95
Everyday Law Made E-Z	BK311		$29.95
Everyday Legal Forms & Agreements	BK307		$29.95
★ **Labor Posters**			
Federal Labor Law Poster	LP001		$11.99
State Labor Law Poster (specify state)			$29.95
★ SHIPPING & HANDLING*			$
★ **TOTAL OF ORDER**:**			$

ss 1999.r2

Index